Getting Personal Using Videoclips
Watch, Listen and Read

Clara Birnbaum／高山一郎 編著

大学生のための
ビデオクリップ英語総合学習

松柏社

DVD 完備

Introduction

Getting Personal is a university-level English course featuring original video and reading material with a very natural, personal flavor. The book treats a variety of interesting and thought-provoking themes from the spectrum of everyday experience, and uses authentic English that is nonetheless accessible and friendly for learners.

While the overall aim is to build general language competence, extra attention is given to listening fluency. The rhythmic quality of English, so different from oral Japanese, makes listening one of the greatest challenges for Japanese learners. Aspects of English rhythm, such as **stress**, **intonation**, and **linking**, are not generally featured in English courses, so we have chosen to do so systematically in a section called **All That Jazz**, in each chapter of the book. This section, along with a listening **True or False**, a **Dictation** and **Comprehension Check**, in support of the **Videoclip**, should help boost students' overall listening ability. These sections account for 6 of the 12 sections in each of the 12 chapters.

A main section in each chapter is the **Introductory Reading** (followed by a **True or False**) which complements the **Videoclip**, at times in mutual support, at other times, by taking a different angle. This, hopefully, will inspire thoughtful exploration of the topic.

Two other sections, **Vocabulary Check** and **Useful Expressions**, are designed to facilitate comprehension of the **Introductory Reading** and **Videoclip**, and also to clarify the wider meaning of the targeted words so students can add them to their working vocabulary.

The **Take Five** section offers the students a chance to take a break. Continuing in the overall theme of each chapter, it features such things as quizzes, puzzles, and poetry.

Finally, the **Expansion Questions** section invites the students to carry each chapter's theme a thoughtful step further in any one of a number of ways; for example, in research, writing, or in discussion.

We hope *Getting Personal* will be a rich and enjoyable experience in English learning for all of you.

Clara Birnbaum / Ichiro Takayama

はしがき

　Getting Personal はオリジナルのビデオクリップとリーディングの教材を特徴とする大学生用の英語教材です。このテキストは、日常的な経験から集めた、さまざまな面白いテーマを扱い、自然な英語を使っていますが、英語は学習者に親しみやすく、十分な理解がし易いものになっています。

　英語の力全体を伸ばすのが本書の目的ですが、特にリスニングに慣れてもらえるように配慮しています。日本語とは非常に異なり、英語はリズム重視の言葉です。このため、英語の聞き取りは日本人の学習者にとって最も難しいポイントのひとつです。しかし、英語のリズムの要素である強勢、抑揚、リンキングなどが授業で取り上げられることはほとんどありません。そこで、本書では12の各章に**All that Jazz**というセクション設け、この重要な要素を体系的に取り上げてみました。このセクションは、ビデオクリップの視聴や**Dictation**のセクションと同様に英語の聞き取りの力の向上に役立つはずです。

　本書 の各章は**All that Jazz**を含む12のセクションから成り、すべてのセクションが章ごとに設けられた同じテーマに関係しています。各章の主となるセクションは、**Introductory Reading**とビデオクリップですが、これらは、お互いを補い合い、同じテーマを別の視点から見ることができるように作られています。この組み合わせによって、学習者がそれぞれのテーマについての考えを深める視野を広げるのに役立つことを願っています。

　セクションのなかには**Introductory Reading**の英文とビデオクリップの理解を助けるのに役立つ問題もあります。例えば語彙のセクションがそのひとつですが、ここではさらに、対象の語彙の広い意味を明らかにし、使える語彙を増やすことができます。

　Take Fiveのセクションはその名前が示すとおり、休憩のためのセクションです。このセクションも章全体のテーマに沿っていますが、ここではゲームやクイズが楽しめます。

　最後の**Expansion Questions** のセクションでは章のテーマについてさらに深く考えてもらいます。いろいろなやり方があります。個人ならばリサーチをしたり、エッセイを書いたり、またグループであればディスカッションをするとよいでしょう。

　Getting Personal で英語の学習を楽しんでください。

　もともとこの教科書で使われている"Getting Personal"というビデオクリップは松柏社から2000年に出版された *Information, Please!* と *More Information, Please!* のなかのリスニング教材の一部でした。これらの教科書は立教大学英語教育研究室が製作し、2006年までReading and Listeningの授業で使用されました。製作プロジェクトでは高山一郎が企画と演出を担当し、クララ・バンバムをはじめとする立教大学英語嘱託講師のチームがスクリプトの執筆とナレーションを担当しました。

　今回の教科書 *Getting Personal* は映像を使ってさまざまなスキルを養成する総合教材として新しい形で出版されることになりましたが、オリジナルのタイトルを受け継ぐことにし

ました。このタイトルは文化や社会問題を教える際に個人的なアプローチが非常に有効であるというわたしたちの考えを反映しているからです。

　本書の出版にあたり、映像の使用を許可してくださった立教大学英語教育研究室と映像製作に参加した以下のみなさんに深く感謝します。イアン・ウィリー、スコット・バーリン、エイドリアン・クラーク、アイコ・トンプソン、エリザベス・ランゲ、リアンドラ・ディートン。また、立教大学で講演を行ったビル・ゲイツ氏とその際にインタビューを担当した鳥飼玖美子教授にもお礼を申し上げます。最後に、松柏社のみなさん、特に編集担当の森有紀子さん、この教科書の完成までご協力いただき、ありがとうございました。

　　2008年12月

クララ・バンバム／高山一郎

Acknowledgements

Originally, the "Getting Personal" videoclips were part of the listening component of two textbooks: *Information, Please!* and *More information, Please!*, published by Shohakusha in 2000. The materials were created by the Rikkyo English Language Program and used in the Reading and Listening Course until 2006. The project involved Ichiro Takayama, as planner and director, and Clara Birnbaum as one member of a team of Rikkyo adjunct lecturers, who wrote and narrated the video segments.

We offer the present textbook *Getting Personal* in its new form as an integrated skills video textbook. The original title is retained because it reflects our belief that a personal approach is an effective way to teach cultural and social issues.

We would like to thank the Rikkyo English Language Program, the owner of the copyright, for its kind permission to use the video segments, and the other writers and narrators of those segments: Ian Willey, Scott Berlin, Adrian Clarke, Aiko Thompson, Elizabeth Lange, and Leandra Deaton. We also thank Bill Gates, and Kumiko Torikai, who interviewed him at Rikkyo University. Finally, we are grateful to the staff at Shohakusha, especially, Yukiko Mori, whose patience and close cooperation was essential in helped bring this project to completion.

Clara Birnbaum / Ichiro Takayama

Contents

Chapter 1 Language: the road to miscommunication 1
  videoclip The Camping Trip

Chapter 2 Big Decisions: the less common path 9
  videoclip A Year Off

Chapter 3 Friendship: the simple joys 17
  videoclip Dear Wendy

Chapter 4 Emotional Health: taking care of ourselves 25
  videoclip Counseling

Chapter 5 The World: travel and tradition 33
  videoclip Korea

Chapter 6 Celebration: sense of community 41
  videoclip An Adventure in Bali

Chapter 7 Giving Birth: the old and the new 49
  videoclip One Woman's Experience

Chapter 8 Music: so basic, so mysterious 57
  videoclip What is Music?

Chapter 9 Gender and Language: hidden sexism 65
  videoclip Gender Language

Chapter 10 Newspapers: different roles 73
  videoclip Newspapers in Britain

Chapter 11 Art: all about life 81
  videoclip On Art

Chapter 12 Information Technology: finding a balance 89
  videoclip An Interview with Bill Gates

Chapter 1

Language:
the road to miscommunication

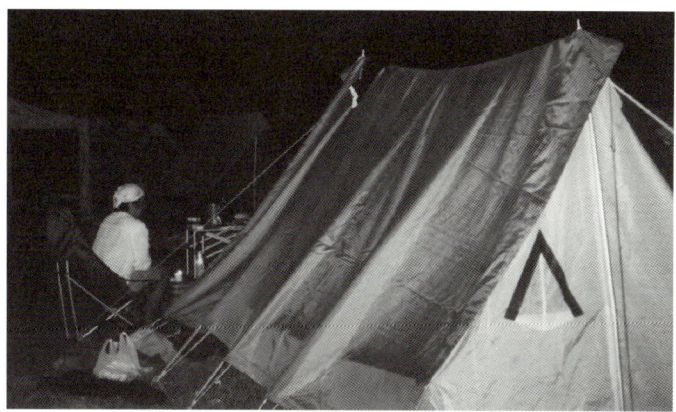

1 Introductory Reading

Read the passage below.

A Little Knowledge

We all speak the language we learned as infants. If we are lucky enough to pick up other languages as well, many doors open for us. However, they say, "a little knowledge can be a dangerous thing". Here's my story.

When I visited China, I was able to read some Chinese because most of the Kanji characters also exist in Japanese and have similar meanings. Once, my train stopped unexpectedly in a remote village. After awhile, I attempted to ask a train worker about the delay by using gesture, simple drawings, and a kanji or two. In response, she wrote down the figure "6" and the Kanji meaning "evening". That would give me several hours to explore the village; maybe visit a teahouse and "chat" with the locals. However, just as I was about to step onto the platform, to my surprise, the train started slowly moving.

I later learned that the Kanji she had written has meanings in Chinese that don't exist in the Japanese. Her message actually said that the train was 6 hours behind schedule. I would possibly still be in that village today if I'd gotten off the train!

In another train-related incident, this time in Europe, a Japanese couple were sold tickets that took them to Genoa instead of to Geneva, because their accents were misunderstood.

It's common for people of different languages to have experiences like these, but we don't expect such misunderstandings amongst speakers of the same language. However, they occur quite regularly. Let's watch this chapter's videoclip in which two friends struggle to communicate together in their first language, English.

(267 words)

2 True or False: Introductory Reading

Answer true (T) or false (F).

1. The writer used non-verbal methods to communicate with the train worker. ( )
2. The writer spent some time visiting a village because the train was delayed. ( )
3. Misunderstandings amongst people of the same language happen often. ( )

3 Vocabulary Check

Fill in the blanks with the words below.

1. If you have a chance to visit this island again, I suggest you (   ) the small villages along the shore by bicycle.
2. In England, the language of communication is English, but there are many different regional (   )s.
3. At the new school, the children had to (   ) with a whole range of unfamiliar subjects, different customs, and new rules.
4. The (   ) had just learned to walk, but made it all the way to the table.
5. The public transportation system is not reliable in this country. A (   ) of one hour is not unusual.
6. We'll be doing a lot of walking on this trip, so we're not bringing heavy (   ).
7. I would love to spend a whole week in a (   ) village in the English countryside away from the rat race.
8. In terms of vocabulary, Chinese and Japanese are (   ), but their grammars are different.
9. When I moved to Bolivia there were a few embarrassing (   )s at first because of cultural differences, but I got used to things eventually.
10. (   ) is obtained from very deep in the ground. From this substance gasoline is produced.

infant, similar, remote, delay, explore, incident, accent, struggle, luggage, petroleum

4 First Viewing: "The Camping Trip"

Watch the videoclip.

5 True or False: videoclip

Listen to each sentence. Check true (T) or false (F).

1. T ☐ F ☐
2. T ☐ F ☐
3. T ☐ F ☐
4. T ☐ F ☐
5. T ☐ F ☐

6 All that Jazz: listening tips

A feature of rhythm, in oral conversational English, is stress. Sometimes unstressed sounds are short and weak, and almost disappear. Sometimes they blend together and make new sounds, as in the following examples.

EXAMPLES:

written English	conversational English
What did you do? >	Whadja do?
Did you eat? >	Didja eat?
Why don't you call her? >	Why don'tcha call her?
Could you open the door? >	Couldja open the door?
Would you come here? >	Wouldja come here?

Listen and complete this conversation in written English.

Sam: (watching a game on TV) Wow! _____
    that? What a goal!!! . . . Julia . . . ?
Julia: (in the next room) _____ me, honey? I
    can't hear you.

Getting Personal

Sam: Julia, Where are you? Why _____ and
   watch the game with me? You had a hard day.
Julia: _____? _____
   that again?
Sam : . . . Can't hear you, Julia . . . _____?
Julia : Geez, Sam . . . _____ the volume down? I
   CAN'T HEAR YOU!!!.

7 Second Viewing

Watch the videoclip again.

8 Comprehension Check: videoclip

Write an answer for each question.

1. Where is Ian from?

_____

2. What word does Ian use to describe the luggage section of the car?

_____

3. What does Adrian mean when he says "cheers" to Ian?

_____

4. Ian calls a certain snack "chips". What is it for Adrian?

_____

Chapter 1 —— Language   5

9 Dictation

Listen and complete each sentence.

1. Did you remember (   ) (   ) (   )?
2. Yeah, I filled up the tank. (   ) (   ) (   ).
3. (   ) (   ) (   ) (   ) chips?

10 Useful Expressions

Complete each sentence with the appropriate word.

1. Hurry up! We're two hours (   ) schedule.
   A. behind   B. on   C. back   D. along
2. I don't (   ) it. Could you try explaining it again?
   A. make   B. put   C. miss   D. get
3. (   ) to buy some milk when you go shopping this evening.
   A. Mind   B. Remember   C. Sure   D. Please
4. We're all (   ) to start. Is everybody here?
   A. put   B. cut   C. set   D. met

Take Five: let's take a break

Join the words in the British English column with the words in the American English column that have the same meaning.

British English	American English
1. biscuit	sidewalk
2. jumper	subway
3. crisps	apartment
4. boot	police officer
5. chemist	cookie
6. pavement	trunk
7. lorry	pants
8. lift	sweater
9. petrol	scarf
10. muffler	druggist
11. trousers	elevator
12. torch	chips
13. flat	flashlight
14. constable	gas
15. underground	truck

12 Expansion Questions

1. What are some regional styles of Japanese spoken in various parts of Japan? Discuss vocabulary and other differences. Can you give an example of the dialect of your home town?
2. Do you use any language expressions with friends that older people may not understand? If so, give some examples.

Chapter 1 ——— Language   7

Big Decisions:
the less common path

CLASSIFIED ADS

OPPORTUNITIES ABROAD

Teaching in Asia

(JAPAN)

Enjoy a fulfilling career!
Explore another culture!

Features Academy is now hiring English teachers for next year. Openings for experienced teachers at all levels. Lucrative salary and good working conditions. Housing provided. For details, contact our overseas office at (Tel) 42-8738-9420.

1 Introductory Reading

Read the passage below.

Pools and Mirrors

Annie dreamed of someday spending a year in Asia, but never did anything to make it happen. One afternoon, as a joke, she answered an ad for a teaching job in Japan, and to her surprise, was accepted, just like that. However, she thought she'd turn the offer down because of all the complications. "Next year perhaps."

"Why don't you go?" her friend asked, surprised. "What will change by next year?"

Annie lay awake that night, tense, thinking about whether to go or not, but by morning felt no closer to a decision. Dreaming of adventure was easy, but making it happen was an unexpected challenge for her. Was she so afraid of change? Maybe her friend was right that next year would be no different.

During the next week Annie was often lost in thought, but eventually she began to relax and to feel that she would be able to handle her fears. Adventure called out to her again, in a clear voice.

She accepted the job in Japan and began one of the most important chapters of her life. It was like dipping into a pool and discovering the wonders of a fascinating and complex culture. It was like gazing into a mirror and seeing, with fresh eyes, who she was and where she was from.

Annie had almost given up going. It would have been a decision based on fear, and she knows in her heart she would have regretted it always. In a similar spirit, Adrian, in the videoclip, embarked on his own adventure. What would you do for a year if you had the chance?

(270 words)

2 True or False: Introductory Reading

Answer true (T) or false (F).

1. Annie started to prepare for Japan as soon as she learned she was hired. (　)
2. Her friend thought she should go to Japan the following year instead. (　)
3. Annie's decision to go to Japan was based on fear and regret. (　)

3 Vocabulary Check

Fill in the blanks with the words below.

1. Our dream of a pleasant relaxing holiday turned into a (　　　).
2. My parents will allow me to travel around Europe, (　　　) that I go with a friend.
3. The queens in fairytales often (　　　) at themselves in the mirror.
4. Water supply is crucial if we hold this event in the (　　　).
5. He's now opposed to the project, but (　　　) he'll come to accept it.
6. They wanted to get married on Mt. Fuji, but there were so many (　　　)s involved, so they decided not to do it.
7. The company will (　　　) on a new project in an effort to increase its market.
8. When I started the course, I was full of (　　　), but I soon got bored.
9. There are many non-governmental (　　　)s that aim to help people who live in poverty.
10. It's a good idea to have a (　　　) plan before reserving accommodation and transportation.

---

organization, desert, eventually, definite, embark, nightmare, provided, complication, enthusiasm, gaze

4 First Viewing: "A Year Off"

Watch the videoclip.

Notes epic 48-hour bus journeys：壮大な48時間のバス旅行　accountant：会計士

5 True or False: videoclip

Listen to each sentence . Check true (T) or false (F).

1.　　T ☐　F ☐
2.　　T ☐　F ☐
3.　　T ☐　F ☐
4.　　T ☐　F ☐
5.　　T ☐　F ☐

6 All that Jazz: listening tips

When "when" isn't a question

In the videoclip, Adrian says that many students take a year off before starting university. He adds, "there are many organizations which help students to decide what to do during that year." Can you find 2 "WH" words in that sentence? They are: <u>which</u> and <u>what</u>.

In such a sentence, WH words are NOT stressed. However, when they are used as question words, they ARE stressed. **Example:** *"Which coat is yours?"*

Exercise:
In the following sentences underline the WH words and add the missing question mark or period at the end. Then read the sentences aloud. Stress the WH words when they are questions, but otherwise, do not stress them. Then listen.

1. Where is the nearest post office (　)
2. Let me tell you why I don't like her very much (　)
3. How do you turn off this computer (　)
4. She learned how to drive when she was only 13 years old (　)
5. When I arrived, I was so tired I fell asleep on the sofa where the cat always sleeps (　)
6. When will he be back (　)

12   Getting Personal

7. If you ask me where I want to live, I'll say I'm happy right where I am ( )
8. Of all the students who applied to Oxford, who do you think will make it ( )
9. Which would you prefer, wine or beer ( )
10. I'll tell you what I want for my birthday only if you tell me what you want for yours ( )

7 Second Viewing

Watch the videoclip again.

8 Comprehension Check: videoclip

Write an answer for each question.

1. Why did Adrian work at a bank after finishing high school?

2. Who did Adrian go to India with?

3. How did Adrian change physically as a result of his trip?

4. What was his attitude about studying when he came home?

9 Dictation

Listen and complete each sentence.

1. Now, many British universities allow students (   ) (   ) (   ) (   ) (   ) university (   ) (   ) (   ).
2. I had to learn how to cook, clean, do the washing, and so on—all things (   ) (   ) used to (   ) (   ) (   ) when I lived at home.
3. I think that taking a year off is a great idea, provided (   ) (   ) (   ) (   ) (   ).

10 Useful Expressions

Complete each sentence with the appropriate word.

1. It was so hot that we took a (   ) for half an hour.
   A. relax   B. break   C. care   D. stop
2. Don't (   ) it for granted that your novel will be published. That happens rarely.
   A. make   B. put   C. keep   D. take
3. Somehow we (   ) to understand what the foreigner was saying.
   A. managed   B. succeeded   C. handled   D. relied
4. Who would have thought I'd have a chance to live in Paris for so long. It was a (   ) come true.
   A. dream   B. time   C. trip   D. desire

11 Take Five: let's take a break

Chain game

1. *The following 6 sentences are in scrambled word order. Unscramble them.*

   A) wife, and, travel, his, plan, Nancy, abroad, he, to
   _____

   B) delicious, from, ate, they, year, that, last, country, ones
   _____

   C) Nancy, about, are, the, however, excited, and, apricots, really, Paul
   _____

   D) many, visit, there, this, other, are, reasons, to, surely, country
   _____

   E) summer, his, forward, is, Paul, looking, to, holidays, really
   _____

   F) grows, Nancy, that, their, to, country, flight, apricots, booked, a
   _____

2. *Change the order of the sentences into a more logical order to make a little story.*

   1 ____ 2 ____ 3 ____ 4 ____ 5 ____ 6 ____

3. *Find the correct word from each sentence using these hints.*
   - from sentence **A**: a joining word: (   )
   - from sentence **B**: a verb: (   )
   - from sentence **C**: a fruit: (   )
   - from sentence **D**: an amount: (   )
   - from sentence **E**: a person: (   )
   - from sentence **F**: a person: (   )

4. Make a sentence using the words in #3: **Paul** _____

5. What country did they visit? To find out, write the first letter of each word in #4 on this line: _____

6. What do you know about this country? Write T (true) or F (false) in the blanks.

   This place……
   ____ connects Central and South America.
   ____ is the same name as a style of hat.
   ____ is a German-speaking country.
   ____ is on the Mediterranean sea.
   ____ is larger than Japan.
   ____ was invaded by the USA.
   ____ has a canal.
   ____ is an Islamic country.
   ____ has both lowlands and mountains.

12 Expansion Questions

1. Would you like to take a year off before starting your working life? If so, how would you want to spend it? If not, explain your reasons.
2. It is said, in Japan, that some companies tend to not favor people taking a year off, or spending 5 or 6 years as undergraduates. What do you think are the reasons, and what is your opinion of this situation?

Friendship:
the simple joys

1 Introductory Reading

Read the passage below.

The Secret Ingredient

Hana was looking forward to meeting Tom because she loved music and Tom was a professional classical singer, but she also felt a little shy and anxious because she wasn't a professional anything. Well, they liked each other immediately and chatted for hours, covering everything from their favorite foods, to their children, politics, and stories from their childhoods.

Of course they also talked about music, and the hours passed like minutes. Hana told Tom about a wonderful CD she had heard at her friend's house the day before. It was classical arrangements of old folksongs, sung by several different singers. She didn't know the album's title. There was one particular song that touched Hana deeply because of its quiet, sad beauty, and she hummed a phrase for Tom. "Do you know it?" she asked. He answered that indeed he did, because he happened to be the one singing that song on the CD! This delightful coincidence added a touch of sweetness to their relationship that had only just begun. By the way, Tom was 74 years old and Hana was 29.

What is the secret ingredient that brings friends together despite age differences and other complicating factors? In this chapter's videoclip, we'll meet two friends with a similar bond to Hana's and Tom's. Because the two in the video are the same age and sex, their close friendship may appear more usual, but in fact, it is made of the same magic. What do you think makes some friendships so "delicious"?

(251 words)

2 True or False: Introductory Reading

Answer true (T) or false (F).

1. Hana was worried because she didn't like music. (　)
2. Hana and Tom chatted about many things, including music. (　)
3. Tom wrote the song that really moved Hana. (　)

3 Vocabulary Check

Fill in the blanks with the words below.

1. A strong (　　) developed amongst the actors while working on the play.
2. The (　　) of the festival for me was watching the many energetic people carrying a huge, portable shrine.
3. We were (　　)d how crowded the trains could be during rush hour in Japan.
4. Children love blowing (　　)s and watching them float up until they burst.
5. The president was (　　)d for his courage but criticized for his inflexibility.
6. I usually buy powder cleanser because the bottles of (　　) are too heavy to carry.
7. When the boy told us about his adventure in the forest, his eyes (　　)d with excitement.
8. The couple will probably (　　) because they argue constantly.
9. He drank a lot of wine at the party and started telling (　　) jokes.
10. On the same day that I sent a postcard to Wendy, I got one from her. It was such a (　　).

> coincidence, bond, amaze, part, silly, highlight, admire, liquid, bubble, sparkle

4 First Viewing: "Dear Wendy"

Watch the videoclip.

Notes   amber：琥珀色の

5 True or False: videoclip

Listen to each sentence. Check true (T) or false (F).

1.   T ☐   F ☐
2.   T ☐   F ☐
3.   T ☐   F ☐
4.   T ☐   F ☐
5.   T ☐   F ☐

6 All that Jazz: listening tips

1.   Telegrams

Telegrams used to be the quickest way to send a message. People kept them short though, because the price was determined by the number of words. To include all the original words could cost about twice the price.

EXAMPLE: "Start trip, South England, Saturday. Back end August. Love, Wendy, Clara"

Listen to the original message and write the words that were dropped.

"(   ) start (   ) trip (   ) South England (   ) Saturday. (   ) (   ) (   ) (   ) back (   ) (   ) end (   ) August. Love, Wendy (   ) Clara"

2.   Telegrams are a little like oral English

In oral English, as in telegrams, the words that carry most of the meaning (nouns, verbs, adjectives, and adverbs) are stressed, and the structure words (pronouns, prepositions, etc) though important, are usually unstressed.

EXAMPLE: "**Wendy shook** her **bottle** and **bubbles formed**, and they **sparkled** in the **light**."

EXAMPLES:

EXERCISE:
Underline the meaning words in the following news report. Then read the full report aloud with stress as needed. The meaning words would be sufficient to express the basic message of this report in a telegram. Then listen.

> Wendy and Clara were found in a deep sleep in an inn near Stonehenge on Tuesday. Two tiny bottles of brandy were lying unopened on the floor next to the beds. It is believed that they got drunk on laughter.

7 Second Viewing

Watch the videoclip again.

8 Comprehension Check: videoclip

Write an answer for each question.

1. Why are Clara and Wendy such good friends? Give at least one reason.

2. Why did Clara buy bottles of brandy?

3. Where did Clara buy the brandy?

4. What did Clara and Wendy do with the bottles?

9 Dictation

Listen and complete each sentence.

1. And yet whenever we meet, we just continue (　　) (　　) we (　　) (　　).
2. The highlight of (　　) (　　) was (　　) (　　) (　　) (　　) fine French brandy.
3. We were (　　) (　　) on (　　) (　　) (　　) we never even opened the bottles.

10 Useful Expressions

Complete each sentence with the appropriate word.

1. The story of finding her lost child (　　) us deeply.
   A. made　　B. touched　　C. held　　D. kept
2. She felt at (　　) surrounded with people she knew.
   A. well　　B. comfort　　C. fine　　D. ease
3. She (　　) to be very talkative when she's nervous.
   A. gains　　B. marks　　C. tends　　D. goes
4. I can't believe it. You must be (　　).
   A. kidding　　B. getting　　C. going　　D. telling

11 Take Five: let's take a break

You will now be a poet. Today you will compose acrostic poems. Read the following example to discover what an acrostic poem is.

> **H**appy, crazy guy.
> **I**s that him again break dancing,
> **R**ight there in front of the glass doors of Building 5?
> **O**ften he's there even during classes, even until midnight.

In the example above, the name "Hiro" was used to write the poem. The 4 letters, written vertically, each began a line of the poem. Acrostic poems don't have strict rules; about grammar, about rhythm, about anything. The only rule is to have fun using your imagination. In the following example, the word "friend" is used. Someone has moved far away from their lover.

Far away again
Rented room, strange voices
I think of you
Each moment is filled with you
Never ending
Distant dream

Now it's your turn. Try these words. Why not also think up some of your own?

1. S
   I
   L
   L
   Y

2. M
   A
   G
   I
   C

12 Expansion Questions

1. What are some important qualities for you in a good friendship? What can make a friendship last or break up?
2. How is life without friends? Do you think it's necessary to have many friends or is one good friend enough?

Chapter 4

Emotional Health:
taking care of ourselves

Introductory Reading

Read the passage below.

A Page from a Diary

I'm not going to class and I don't care. It's comfortable under this old tree. Nobody laughs at you here, and teachers don't ask you questions you can't answer while forty faces stare at you. They all seem so cool here and I just don't fit in. I really hate being at school and I don't know how long I can continue like this. What if I do something really stupid? I don't care really, but what about my parents? I love this old tree and the feel of its ancient bark. It's somehow soft and warm to the touch.

A gentle wind is dancing through its branches, and the sun is soft and warm, but none of that can penetrate my heart that is like a rock.

I have stood here with my spread out branches for almost a century, watching the students pass under me day-by-day. I look into their young hearts, and see their simple joys and hopes, and also their hidden fears. They glance secretly at the others, wishing they could be as confident, hiding their loneliness in playful chatter. I cry out to them in my silence, "You are unique," but they don't hear me. Perhaps they don't want to. My leaves reach out but are like wings that can't fly. That sad, young man, for instance, has been sitting on the bench since lunchtime, writing in his diary. If only I could hold him in my arms, and tell him that he is not alone. He is like the others; perfect, just as he is. I think, one day, when he is older, he will come to realize that.

2 True or False: Introductory Reading

Answer true (T) or false (F).

1. The student writing his diary thinks teachers generally ask hard questions. (　)
2. He wishes the weather would improve. (　)
3. The tree would like to tell the students they are all special and unique. (　)

3 Vocabulary Check

Fill in the blanks with the words below.

1. Why do they always (　　)? Can't they agree about anything?
2. Our neighbor's music is so loud that it (　　)s the thick walls and keeps us awake.
3. Professor Kim was my (　　). We met every month to go over my research.
4. The course was too (　　), so many of the students failed the exam.
5. If the police can't find the missing person, we can hire a private (　　).
6. Because of the (　　) look on her face, we didn't realize she was joking.
7. As they say, "No pain, no (　　)", so stop complaining and get down to work!
8. The cause of the pain is not physical but (　　). It's all in your mind.
9. I just happened to (　　) at the far table in the restaurant and saw my boyfriend with another woman.
10. We visited a haunted castle in a remote village. It was so (　　).

penetrate, glance, psychological, argue, serious, scary, supervisor, demanding, detective, gain

Chapter 4 —— Emotional Health　27

4 First Viewing: "Counseling"

Watch the videoclip.

5 True or False: videoclip

Listen to each sentence. Check true (T) or false (F).

1. T ☐ F ☐
2. T ☐ F ☐
3. T ☐ F ☐
4. T ☐ F ☐
5. T ☐ F ☐

6 All that Jazz: listening tips

Tag Questions

A tag question is a statement with a little question tagged onto the end. It is part statement and part question, and its meaning is somewhere between the two.

EXAMPLES:

1. He lives in Paris, doesn't he?
    positive   negative

2. She doesn't eat meat, does she?
    negative   positive

Notice that if the main part of the sentence is positive, the tagged part is negative. If the main part is negative, the tagged part is positive.

POINT: *There are 2 kinds of tag questions:*

In the 1st kind, the question ends in an up tone:

EXAMPLE: **A:** That coffee shop is good, isn't it? ↗ **B:** It's great. Try it. You'll like it.

In the 2nd kind, the question ends in a down tone:

EXAMPLE: **A:** That coffee shop is good, isn't it? ↘ **B:** You're so right. I love it too.

*In the 1st example, **A** has never been to the coffee shop but has heard it is good. The question is to confirm that it is good. In the 2nd one, **A** <u>has</u> been to the shop and is giving an opinion about it.*

28   Getting Personal

*Although it looks like a question, it is mainly a statement with some question feeling in the sense that **A** expects **B** to respond. (In the simple statement: "That coffee shop is good", **A** does not necessarily expect **B** to respond.)*

EXERCISE:
Make tag questions by adding a tag to each statement. Read each question, with an up tone, then down. See if you can understand the difference. Then listen.

1. You keep a diary, _____?
2. This book is about depression, _____?
3. Ms. Lee, the counselor, comes on Tuesdays, _____?
4. They loved each other, _____?
5. There's a shortage of counselors, _____?
6. Ann doesn't need medication, _____?
7. He isn't lonely, _____?
8. You feel better now, _____?
9. It would be better to tell her, _____?
10. You can see I'm sad, _____?

7 Second Viewing

Watch the videoclip again.

8 Comprehension Check: videoclip

Write an answer for each question.

1. Why did the woman become a counselor?

_____

2. What are one or two examples of "normal" problems, according to the woman?

_____

3. What does the woman compare counseling work to?

4. What lesson did the woman gain from her experience?

9 Dictation

Listen and complete each sentence.

1. You've had (   ) experience (   ) (   ) counselor, (   ) (   )?
2. Oh, that's quite a big range of problems. It must (   ) been (   ) (   ) (   ) (   ).
3. Someone will come to you and tell you what their problem is. But it's (   ) (   ) (   ) as a counselor (   ) (   ) (   ) (   ) (   ) information.

10 Useful Expressions

Complete each sentence with the appropriate word.

1. Don't worry. You'll soon (   ) in with others and make some friends.
   A. come   B. fit   C. stay   D. get
2. What (   ) I fail? I'm really anxious about this exam.
   A. about   B. come   C. if   D. only
3. She tried to (   ) out to the young, sad boy but without success.
   A. throw   B. pull   C. bring   D. reach
4. It is (   ) to each of us to choose how we will live our lives.
   A. off   B. down   C. up   D. on

11 Take Five: let's take a break

Message in a Bottle

You have probably heard of people tossing a bottle into the sea with a message inside. This romantic activity has existed, no doubt, since the beginning of bottles. We can't know where it will end up, but hopefully someone will find it and respond.

Imagine you will send such a bottle off to sea. Write your message as a diary entry, expressing any feelings, hopes, and worries you have about your life at university and after you leave. Be open and honest, but only share what you are comfortable sharing, BECAUSE, someone will find the bottle!!

Write your diary entry in the bottle on the following page.

12 Expansion Questions

1. Is your university life an emotional challenge? Compare it to your high school life. Which is more stressful and why? What are some good ways to deal with stress?
2. In some cultures people are advised to endure painful emotions quietly and not complain about them or consult others. Give your thoughts about this.

32 Getting Personal

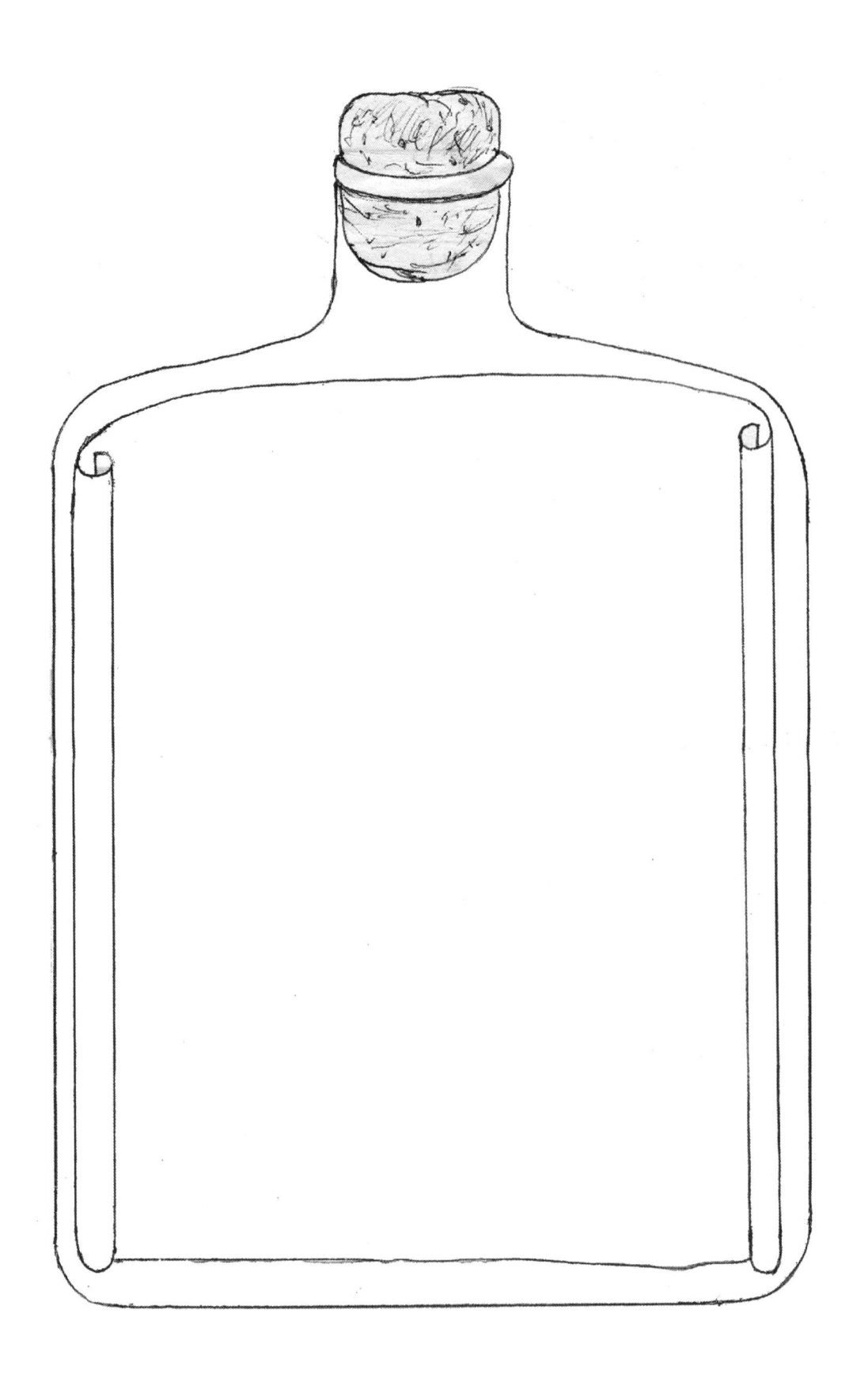

Chapter 5

The World:
travel and tradition

1 Introductory Reading

Read the passage below.

Bridges and Gates

The old bridge in Mostar, Bosnia-Herzegovena, was a strikingly beautiful stone arch over the Neretva river. It linked, not only the two shores of the rushing river, but also several cultural communities that lived on opposite sides, so it stood as a bridge of social unity as well. When it was destroyed in the hostilities of the early 1990's, the wound was very deep.

Seoul suffered a similar tragedy when its national treasure, Namdae Mun, was destroyed by fire. In this chapter's videoclip, you will see the great gate sitting quietly in the middle of a multi-lane highway, watching the centuries pass by. In the space of a day, it was gone.

Like humans, a nation finds its identity by weaving threads of connection through the present and past. The world is moving so fast and it is very easy to lose sense of place and history. The spirit suffers when these ties are lost. Ancient buildings and monuments are solid links with the past, and when they are destroyed it is as though the country's own roots have been violently pulled out of the ground.

Mostar's bridge was rebuilt, in part from stones of the old bridge that were found at the bottom of the river. The old city now looks very much as it did for centuries before the war. Perhaps like Mostar, Seoul will decide to rebuild Namdae Mun to be a perfect likeness of the old gate. Maybe it will choose another healing path instead. The most important thing however, is that the spirit of connectedness, symbolized by Namdae Mun, not be broken.

(268 words)

2 True or False: Introductory Reading

Answer true (T) or false (F).

1. The bridge in Mostar kept the different communities apart. ( )
2. Historical monuments can be a strong connection between the past and present. ( )
3. Some of the original stones were used to rebuild the new Namdae Mun. ( )

3 Vocabulary Check

Fill in the blanks with the words below.

1. In order to graduate from this university you will have to earn 125 (   )s.
2. That school tries to (   ) the teaching of the language skills. In other words, they're not taught separately.
3. There was so much (   ) between the two neighbors that one of them finally decided to move away.
4. There was a rumor of a lot of hidden (   ) on this island.
5. In (   ) times many kinds of arts and crafts came to Japan by way of Korea.
6. The earthquake was a huge (   ) and thousands of people suffered.
7. Traffic is moving very slowly along the main highway because of a big accident in the left (   ).
8. I think Tom and Kate will (   ) up because he thinks she's too conservative.
9. In the past there were more solid (   )s between the generations because they lived under the same roof.
10. I don't buy this magazine because it has so many (   )s and so few articles.

> hostility, tragedy, lane, tie, advertisement, credit, integrate, treasure, split, ancient

4　First Viewing: "Korea"

Watch the videoclip.

Notes　cucumber：きゅうり

5　True or False: videoclip

Listen to each sentence. Check true (T) or false (F).

1. T ☐　F ☐
2. T ☐　F ☐
3. T ☐　F ☐
4. T ☐　F ☐
5. T ☐　F ☐

6　All that Jazz: listening tips

1. *Read the following lines aloud. Do some take more time to say than others?*

Rose sells beets

1. Rose sells beets.
2. She also sells carrots and lettuce,
3. She sells cabbage on Sundays and Tuesdays,
4. and she sometimes sells plums on a Friday.
5. If you're lucky you'll also find flowers.
6. She has lilies, and daisies, and posies,
7. but my favorites are clearly the roses.

You may be surprised to learn that all 7 lines take the same amount of time to say because they have the same number of stressed or strong sounds (marked in bold below). In English, a rhythm language, the stressed sounds "keep the beat", and the other sounds, which are weak, are said in between. If there are many other sounds, they simply are said more quickly. Now listen.

1.	**Rose**	**sells**	**beets**.
2. She	**al**so sells	**car**rots and	**let**tuce,
3. She sells	**cab**bage on	**Sun**days and	**Tues**days,
4. and she	**some**times sells	**plums** on a	**Fri**day.

36　Getting Personal

5. If you're **luc**ky you'll **al**so find **flow**ers;
6. She has **li**lies, and **dai**sies, and **po**sies,
7. but my **fa**vorites are **clear**ly the **ro**ses.

2. In the videoclip, Scott says this sentence. (Notice that the stressed words express most of the meaning.)

"**Af**ter I **grad**uated, I re**ceived** a **phone** call from a **friend** of mine who was **liv**ing and **work**ing in Kor**e**a at that time."

EXERCISE:
In the following sentence, the stressed words are given, and the unstressed words are missing. Listen, and fill in the blanks.

_____ original plan _____ _____ work _____ _____ one year, _____ _____ ended _____ working _____ _____ _____ 6 _____.

3. Finally, here is a silly poem to end with. It's a limerick, which is a form that gives a strong sense of English rhythm. Try it. Then listen.

Ballad of Sir Scott the Adventurer

Scott's **known** for his **pas**sion for **tra**vel,
The world's **mys**teries he **hopes** to un**ra**vel.
He **cy**cled through **Seoul**,
ended **up** at the **Pole**,
but he **prompt**ly got **stuck** in the **gra**vel.

7 Second Viewing

Watch the videoclip again.

8 Comprehension Check: videoclip

Write an answer for each question.

1. What did Scott do in Korea the first time?

2. What is one aspect of Korean culture that impressed Scott?

_____

3. What does the name Namdae Mun mean in English?

_____

4. What kind of information did the grandmother in the market often give Scott?

_____

9 Dictation

Listen and complete each sentence.

1. Sometimes, (   ) (   ) (   ) (   ) (   ) your life.
2. Now Namdae Mun sits in the heart of Seoul, and it's (   ) (   ) (   ) (   ) (   ) the road.
3. When (   ) (   ) (   ) (   ) from (   ), I would ask for a discount.

10 Useful Expressions

Complete each sentence with the appropriate word.

1. The program at the cultural center is like a (   ) that connects the generations of the community.
   A. bridge   B. cord   C. tape   D. exit
2. The old cat always sits at the window watching the people pass (   ).
   A. by   B. off   C. out   D. up
3. We wanted to camp, but it rained so we (   ) up staying at a hotel.
   A. picked   B. decided   C. ended   D. made

4. If you want to use the special room at the library, ask (   ) permission.

   A. at B. with C. of D. for

11 Take Five: let's take a break

Quick Voyage

This activity is a crossword puzzle. It tests your knowledge of several of the world's famous sites, some natural, some human made. Complete each sentence by writing the name of a country in the grid. Need help? Do the mini puzzle first on the following page.
Super Champion challenge: Try answering the questions without the crossword grid.

ACROSS
1. The Serengeti plains of ( ), Africa, considered "heritage" territory, give protection to many animals, such as giraffes and ostriches, but as human numbers increase, their safety is in danger.
2. Ayuthaya, the rich and busy capital of 15th Century ( ) was destroyed after 2 years of war, and then abandoned and forgotten. It eventually fell to ruin.
3. The Bamyan Buddhas in ( ) were destroyed by the Taliban in 2001. Though the Taliban fell from power in the war that followed 9-11, still there is no peace in this country.
4. Angkkor Wat in ( ), a forgotten masterpiece of Kmer architecture, was lost under jungle growth for a long time. It was later rediscovered but eventually suffered great damage during the civil war of the 1970's.
5. Because earthquakes are frequent in this area of ( ), the Parthenon and other nearby sites are undergoing protective measures to keep them safe.
6. Although there was severe damage to some heritage sites in ( ) in the earthquake of 1992, luckily, the Temple of Luxor received only a few cracks.
7. San Gimignano, famous for its many stone towers, is one of many hilltop medieval towns in ( ). It is surrounded by beautiful rolling country covered in grape and olive orchards.
8. The largest coral reef is in ( ), and is one of the world's richest areas in biodiversity. It is extremely sensitive to climate change and is in great danger today.

DOWN
1. The Taj Mahal, in ( ), was built in the mid 1600's by the Emperor, in loving memory of his wife who died in childbirth.
2. It is believed that the standing stones of Stonehenge in ( ) were placed around 2200 B.C., perhaps as a burial ground. Modern life is not far away. In fact the site is surrounded by traffic.
3. Komodo National Park in ( ) is now, luckily, a world heritage site that offers protection to the

Komodo Dragon, the largest lizard in the world.
4. The old city of Dubrovnick, in ( ) was badly damaged in the attack by Serbia in the early 1990's.
5. The Three Gorges, called the Grand Canyon of ( ), is the site of a major dam. Whether the increase in electricity is worth the high cost to the environment, is a matter of hot debate.
6. Machu Picchu in ( ) is a magnificent old Inca site that was built high up in the mountains around 1450. It is often called the lost city of the Incas.
7. The Galapagos in ( )is home to many unusual animals, including the famous tortoises, the world's longest living animals. These islands are in danger due to large-scale tourism and unsustainable fishing.

> * **Mini puzzle:** If you do this puzzle in the main crossword grid, you will have extra letters to help you do the main puzzle.
>
> **ACROSS**
> A. opposite of "beginning":( )
> B. true ( ) false.
> C. ( )s make honey.
> D. Birds lay ( )s.
> E. a ( ) of coffee
> F. Horses ( ) fast.
> G. I don't mind at ( ).
>
> **DOWN**
> A. Let's go home. It's very ( ).
> B. a pear and ( ) apple
> C. seven, eight, nine, ( )
> D. ( ) and eggs
> E. It's cold. Don't ( ) sick.
> F. I haven't finished ( ).
> G. He ( ) no money.
> H. Japanese green ( )
> I. Please answer ( ) or no.

12 Expansion Questions

1. Imagine that you can spend a full day in Tokyo with a friend coming to visit from abroad. Explain in detail what you would choose to do. (If you don't know Tokyo well, you can choose another place in Japan.)
2. Scott, in the videoclip, mentioned the contrast of old and new in Korea. Do you think Japan shows the same characteristic? Explain.

Chapter 6

Celebration:
sense of community

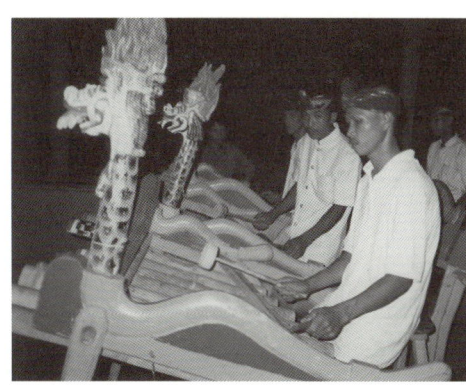

1 Introductory Reading

Read the passage below.

Lost and Found

Why do people travel? There are many reasons of course, but mine are to explore other cultures and landscapes different from my own, and thus, to learn about myself. I also love the unexpected. This article is about that kind of traveling.

If you'd like some advice, I have three simple tips. Go slowly. Go gently. Get lost. With these principles and enough money for one cheap trip, you will be rewarded with a lifetime of memories, something not guaranteed with package tours. Here is one travel story to prove it.

My friend and I were traveling by bicycle in the Tohoku area. We followed country roads that wandered through hills, forests, and rice fields, turning this way and that. The thought even crossed my mind that we were hopelessly lost.

Soon we heard taiko drums and flutes in the distance, and headed in that direction. We reached the edge of a village about to start its summer festival parade, and it was like entering a colorful scene from an Edo period woodcut, with small stalls selling snacks and toys and plastic masks, and people in traditional summer clothing standing around. Soon several men ran up to us and thanked us warmly. "Why?" we asked, and they told us that everyone in the village was in the parade or managing a stall and there was nobody left to simply watch the parade; only us.

This chapter's videoclip relates another adventure full of surprises, and demonstrates, once again, that traveling according to the three basic principles is simply the best way to travel. At least, I think so. (266 words)

2 True or False: Introductory Reading

Answer true (T) or false (F).

1. The writer likes to have a very clear travel goal. (　)
2. The writer and her friend traveled by local country bus and got lost. (　)
3. They were thanked because they bought Edo period woodcuts. (　)

3 Vocabulary Check

Fill in the blanks with the words below.

1. My uncle is very talented and can play eight different musical (　　　)s.
2. People in Europe and America (　　　) their shoulders to express that something cannot be helped.
3. The most magnificent time of day in this region is (　　　) as the light fades behind the mountains.
4. It takes great skill to (　　　) carpets with such complex patterns.
5. The company will (　　　) her for her efforts with a promotion and more pay.
6. (　　　) grows abundantly on this island and is used to make furniture for export.
7. Before you're interviewed for the job, let me give you a few useful (　　　)s.
8. In our group we follow two (　　　)s: honesty and equality.
9. I love her (　　　) voice. What I mean is, it's so mysterious and deep.
10. For our parents' 50th wedding anniversary, we're planning a big (　　　).

> tip, principle, reward, instrument, bamboo, shrug, twilight, weave, haunting, celebration

Chapter 6 ── Celebration 43

4 First Viewing: "An Adventure in Bali"

Watch the videoclip.

Notes   xylophone：木琴   rupia：ルピア（インドネシアの通貨）   sarong：スカートのように腰に巻く布

5 True or False: videoclip

Listen to each sentence . Check true (T) or false (F).

1.   T☐   F☐
2.   T☐   F☐
3.   T☐   F☐
4.   T☐   F☐
5.   T☐   F☐

6 All that Jazz: listening tips

What Mikio Heard

1. One day, in English class, Mikio was confused. When the teacher announced the title of the passage they would read in class that day, Mikio thought he heard "loss tin found". He turned to Ken sitting next to him and asked, "What does 'loss tin found' mean?" Can you guess what the teacher really said? Answer:_____ (If not, please be patient.)

EXPLANATION: *The teacher's pronunciation of the chapter's title included 2 features of spoken English:* 1. **linking:** *Words are often joined together, especially between consonants and vowels. A learner may not know where the two words divide.* (EXAMPLE: *"keep up" sounds like "key pup"*).
2. **reduction:** *Sounds are often dropped. For instance, the word "and", which is unstressed, might sound like /nd/ or even /n/, with no /d/ sound at all.* (EXAMPLE: *"wood and stone" sounds like "wooden stone".*)
Now can you guess what the teacher said to Mikio's class?

2. Look at the word groups below. They are what a listener thought she heard. Try and guess what the speaker really said. (hint: "And" appears in all of them.) Finally, listen and check your answers.

a pin down	weight in sea	sun witch in soup
bay cannon ham	law injustice	lie tin dark
sumo can fire	storeman wind	sadden a loan
Sultan pep her	raw can roll	given take

3. In this chapter's videoclip listen for examples of "and" reduced to /n/ and /nd/. Try saying them.

7 Second Viewing

Watch the videoclip again.

8 Comprehension Check: videoclip

Write an answer for each question.

1. Who is Mono Arta?

2. What did Mono Arta say that disappointed Clara?

3. Who came to the performance besides the men, women, and children?

4. What did Mono Arta do after the concert?

9 Dictation

Listen and complete each sentence.

1. I'd (　　　) (　　　) (　　　) one (　　　) (　　　) (　　　) (　　　) (　　　).
2. (　　　) (　　　) (　　　) everywhere, (　　　) (　　　) (　　　) (　　　), even amongst the instruments.
3. At one point, (　　　) (　　　) (　　　) performed (　　　) (　　　) (　　　) (　　　) with such elegance.

10 Useful Expressions

Complete each sentence with the appropriate word.

1. A good idea (　　　) my mind.
   A. occurred　　**B.** appeared　　**C.** traveled　　**D.** crossed
2. I think we should (　　　) for home now. It's getting late.
   A. head　　**B.** ride　　**C.** go　　**D.** reach
3. It started to rain just as we were (　　　) to leave.
   A. up　　**B.** on　　**C.** off　　**D.** about
4. You look very hungry. Let me (　　　) my sandwich with you.
   A. treat　　**B.** spare　　**C.** share　　**D.** part

11 Take Five: let's take a break

1. *Unscramble the following with the help of the hints. Write the words in the blanks.*

EXAMPLE: vitaslef (a happy event) ___festival___

1. leeppo (more than one person) _____
2. runb (destroy by fire) _____
3. ojyen (feel good) _____
4. memrus (season) _____
5. rumd (an instrument we hit) _____
6. ioihrkas (castle city in Aomori) _____
7. uegh (extremely large) _____
8. telfu (an instrument we blow) _____
9. reppa (material to write on) _____
10. drib (a creature that flies) _____

2. *Complete the following text by filling in the blanks with the appropriate words from the list above.*

Another Festival: Fabulous! Fun! Fantastic!

There are two festivals in Aomori Prefecture which take place at about the same time each year in the middle of (1 _____): Nebuta, in Aomori City, and Neputa in (2 _____). They are quite different from one another, but both are spectacular and lots of fun, and hundreds of (3 _____) from all over the country (4 _____) them very much.

In the case of Neputa, magnificent, very (5 _____) wooden floats in the shape of fans (*sensu*) that are lit-up from inside, are pulled through the streets in the evening, to the melodies of (6 _____)s and the rhythm of (7 _____)s. Their flat surfaces are covered in Japanese (8 _____) painted with colorful scenes of (9 _____)s, beasts, and warriors from old legends. When the festival is over, the floats, that have taken months to create, are (10 _____)ed, and preparation begins all over again for the festival the following year.

Chapter 6 —— Celebration 47

12 Expansion Questions

1. Compare independent travel and package tours. What are their advantages and disadvantages? If you have experienced either one, share some of your memories. If not, which travel style would you choose, and why?
2. Japan is a country that loves festivals. Why do you think this is so? Do you think festivals are as important now as they were in the past? Explain.

Chapter 7

Giving Birth:
the old and the new

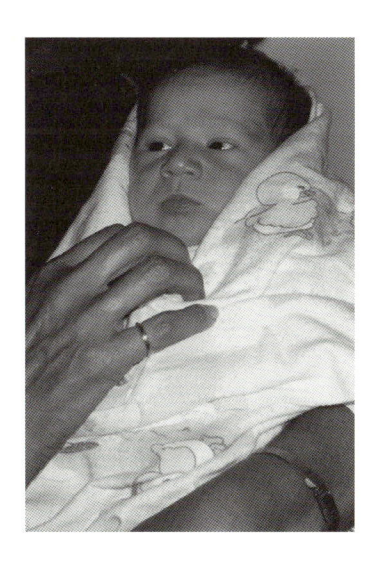

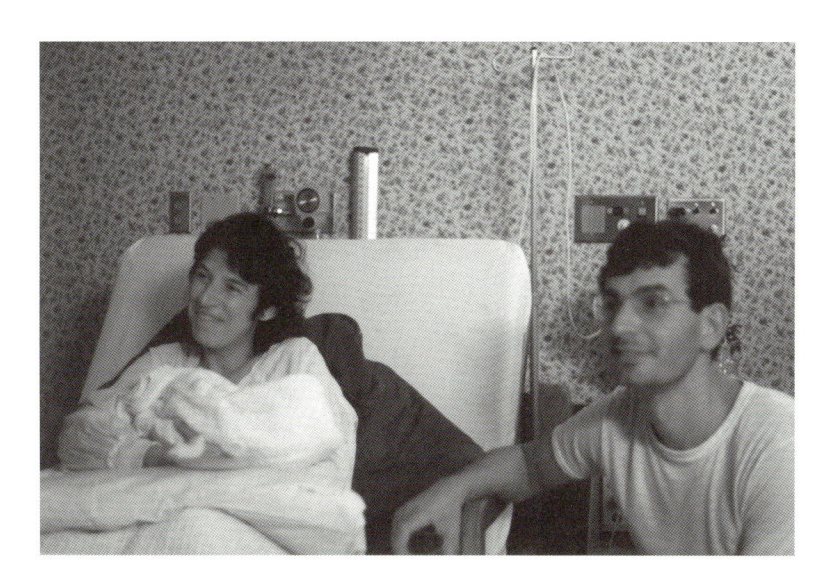

1 Introductory Reading

Read the passage below.

" I'm not sick "

"Why would I go to the hospital?" Freda argued. "I'm not sick or wounded. I'm pregnant." Her mother was urging her to give up thoughts of a natural home birth, and go instead to hospital where they could stop labor pain with medication.

In developed countries, similar conversations are common, but in the past, women simply had babies at home, using natural methods to manage discomfort and pain. Since nature designed the body to endure the physical intensity of pregnancy, most births went smoothly, and women returned to their usual day-to-day after a short rest.

While modern medicine is clearly a blessing in complicated pregnancies, even low-risk births commonly take place in hospital nowadays. Many women nowadays, accustomed to comfort and convenience, choose strong medication, which cuts, not only pain, but all feeling in the lower body. Let's consider the wisdom of this.

Bringing new life into the world is intense; emotionally, spiritually, and physically, and may be nature's way of teaching the mother to put aside her own comfort for the sake of her baby. If the mother thought of the difficult work of labor as a precious gift to both herself and her child, perhaps it would be easier to endure.

We should remember, also, that the pain of normal labor signals the arrival of a new life, not some problem, so is different from the pain of sickness or trauma. Understanding this difference would also diminish the anguish of labor.

Each woman must design her own pregnancy plan. Increasingly, women like Freda, and Aiko in the videoclip, are returning to the age-old option of natural childbirth.

(262 words)

2 True or False: Introductory Reading

Answer true (T) or false (F).

1. Freda wants to have her baby in the hospital. (   )
2. In the past, because women usually gave birth at home, they had to rest a long time. (   )
3. Labor pain is different from the pain we feel when something is wrong. (   )

3 Vocabulary Check

Fill in the blanks with the words below.

1. The doctor gave me some pills to (   ) my headache.
2. One (   ) controversial issue is the use of biofuel as an energy source.
3. I am afraid of (   )s. I try not to look at the needle.
4. The cause of your problem is not (   ) but psychological. I suggest you see a psychiatrist.
5. Sometimes a (   ) woman has an incredible appetite. Perhaps she is eating for two.
6. The (   ) for some illnesses is too expensive for poor people to buy.
7. Don't (   ) my hand so hard! You'll break my bones.
8. "You are (   ) with all the comforts and luxuries imaginable, so stop complaining," the father told the child.
9. He caused his mother such (   ) when he told her that he was leaving and never returning.
10. I can't (   ) my little sister's loud music another minute!

> pregnant, endure, medication, current, physical, squeeze, relieve, agony, injection, blessed

4 First Viewing: "One Woman's Experience"

Watch the videoclip.

Notes   ultrasound picture：超音波診断画像　 womb：子宮　 relaxant：緩和剤　 labor：分娩

5 True or False: videoclip

Listen to each sentence . Check true (T) or false (F).

1.　T ☐　F ☐
2.　T ☐　F ☐
3.　T ☐　F ☐
4.　T ☐　F ☐
5.　T ☐　F ☐

6 All that Jazz: listening tips

When learners misunderstand spoken English, one reason is that a word beginning or ending in a vowel sound often gets "linked" to the word before or after it. Learners can easily make mistakes hearing where words begin and end.   **EXAMPLE:** *"make up" sounds like "may cup"*
(Note: In chapter 6, *All that Jazz* focused on both "linking" and "reduction" in groups of words joined by "and".)

1.   Yoko is working in Chicago

Yoko felt confused about the question her boss had just asked her. She said it in her mind again, "Did you get a plate?" but she still didn't understand. "Oh well," she thought, "One day I'll understand English better." She turned on her computer and got to work.

As she was about to go home at 6, her boss said to her, "Please come on time tomorrow. You were 15 minutes late this morning." "I'm sorry," she replied, and then suddenly she laughed. "Ahhhhh!!! Now I understand what you asked me this morning!"

Her boss had asked, "_____."

52   Getting Personal

2. **EXERCISE**: In English class one day, the teacher played the videoclip, "One Woman's Experience", and told the students to take quick notes as they listened. Sachiko wrote down what she thought she heard. Her notes are on the right. Listen to the following parts from the videoclip. Can you explain Sachiko's mistakes?

The videoclip		Sachiko's quick notes
"when I found out I was pregnant"	>	Aiko doubted pregnant
"see my baby's face, her eyes, and mouth"	>	baby will rise
"after about 12 hours of labor"	>	something rub out
"I finally settled on a few injections"	>	win something

3. **EXERCISE**: Read the following sentences aloud, linking where necessary. In each sentence a learner might hear a wrong word. Can you guess those words from the choices below? Finally, listen to the sentences.

1. She wiped the spilt milk off the table.
2. They're at the bank right now.
3. Look up! There's the North Star right there!
4. Take these pills for your backache.
5. Is this dish made with miso or soy sauce?
6. Could I tell you my little secret?

WORD CHOICES: cake / cough / rat / cup / war / die

7 Second Viewing

Watch the videoclip again.

8 Comprehension Check: videoclip

Write an answer for each question.

1. What did Aiko do to prepare for childbirth? Mention at least one thing.

2. How did Aiko first find out that her baby was a girl?

3. What did Aiko's husband do to help her during labor?

___

4. Why was Aiko happy in the end?

___

9 Dictation

Listen and complete each sentence.

1. When I found out I was pregnant, (   ) (   ) (   ) (   ) preparing (   ) (   ) (   ) body (   ) (   ).
2. During the most painful times, (   ) (   ) (   ) (   ) and (   ).
3. I knew it was going to be painful, but I had no idea (   ) (   ) (   ) last (   ) (   ) labor (   ).

10 Useful Expressions

Complete each sentence with the appropriate word.

1. We built the gate in the garden for the (   ) of the baby.
    A. account   B. case   C. sake   D. chance
2. She decided to prepare for the difficult weeks to (   ) by taking some days off.
    A. arrive   B. come   C. pass   D. meet
3. The doctor advised (   ) drinking too much.
    A. against   B. after   C. off   D. at
4. After a long discussion they (   ) on a compromise.
    A. solved   B. expected   C. reached   D. settled

54   Getting Personal

11 Take Five: let's take a break

In the following crossword puzzle, the theme of birth and babies continues, but other animals besides humans are included. Good luck!

ACROSS
1. When babies are born they're very ( ) for all their needs.
2. There were 3 tiny birds in the ( ) crying for their mother.
3. The baby has started to ( ) and will soon be up and walking.
4. Babe is a famous young ( ) in children's books and movies.
5. Her young teeth are all in now and she can ( ) very well.
6. They're too ( ) to enter the theatre. The minimum age is 6.
7. The tiny ( ) left the other sheep and wandered to the pond.
8. Baby mammals drink the ( ) of their mothers.
9. Please shut the window. It's a little too ( ) for the baby.
10. They live in the country so their child can experience the wonders of ( ).
11. The mother told her child not to ( ) the cookies before lunch.
12. By nature, mothers form a very deep ( ) with their babies.
13. She held the tiny ( ) in her arms and he soon stopped crying.
14. Babies seem so ( ) and innocent when they come into the world.
15. The boss shows great ( ) for the puppy, but not for the workers.
16. The mother ( ) a sweet lullaby to help her baby fall asleep.
17. During the ninth month of her ( ) I stayed with her to help out.

DOWN
1. It won't take long for the ( )s to become frogs.
2. The child planted a pumpkin ( ) in the rose garden.
3. It was moving to see the little ( ) crack through its egg.
4. They will ( ) the walls of the baby's room in bright colors.
5. Interestingly, both human and goat children are called ( )s.

Chapter 7 —— Giving Birth 55

6. Human babies develop in their mother's ( ) for 9 months.
7. Have you ever seen the ( ) of an ostrich? It's huge.
8. The sleepy child lay down with the dog and took a ( ).
9. She took the tiny ( ) home, and her own cat took care of it.
10. It's too ( ) in here for the baby. Please open the window a little.
11. There are 5 children and only the ( ) one, number 3, is a girl.
12. The ( ) kitten grew up to be a fearful, violent cat.
13. Many women choose natural home ( ) instead of having their baby in hospital.
14. In some cultures, babies drink milk from their mother's ( ) for up to 2 years.
15. The 2-year-old identical ( )s have been together since birth.
16. It's almost ( ) so we'd better give the children some lunch.
17. It's hard to believe that the ( ) of such a tiny baby can be so loud.

12 Expansion Questions

1. What are your feelings about taking strong pain medication when giving birth, and about a partner being present at the birth? Answer from your own point of view, as female or male.

2. Do you hope to have children? If so, when would you want to start your family, and how many children (male / female) would you want? What are some of the things adults must consider these days when thinking about starting a family?

Chapter 8

Music:
so basic,
so mysterious

1 Introductory Reading

Read the passage below.

Ancient Medicine

Today's videoclip takes us down an interesting and surprising path when it asks, "What is music?" This simple-looking question inspires lively debate, but what is universal is that we are all touched deeply by music for similar reasons. Let's visit a very far away place and look at the healing side of music.

It's 2005. A truck is traveling along a narrow, dirt road in the war zone of Northern Uganda where rebels may be hiding in the bush. Nevertheless it arrives safely at *Patongo Displacement Camp*, temporary home to 50,000 of the *Acholi* people, forced to leave their nearby farmlands because of the extreme danger. Most have known sadness of a nature we can't imagine: husbands murdered while helpless wives watch, young children taken away and forced to become soldiers. These people manage to live. It's almost a miracle. Thanks, largely to music's power to heal, their spirits are kept alive.

It is for music that the three people in the truck have come. They will help the community prepare for the National Music Competition in the capital, Kampala, 200 miles away. One wouldn't expect poor people in a crowded camp to enter a major competition, but the Acholi are determined. One child explains that music and dance has always been their life, and war can never rob them of it.

Watching them perform in Kampala is proof of music's magic. Their faces look soft, relaxed, and happy, and the audience is delighted. The musicians return to camp, waving their cups proudly. However, the treasure is not the trophies but the music itself, surely the greatest of all medicines.

(270 words)

2   True or False: Introductory Reading

Answer true (T) or false (F).

1. The writer says people everywhere are moved by music, but for different reasons. (   )
2. Life in the camp is difficult because music is not allowed. (   )
3. The musicians from the camp enjoyed the competition, but did not win. (   )

3   Vocabulary Check

Fill in the blanks with the words below.

1. "Stand up. (   ). Sit down." This was a routine we were required to follow right until the end of high school.
2. Marriage is (   ) but the customs and responsibilities can be quite different in each culture.
3. My husband's loving touch was very (   ) and my pain disappeared completely.
4. This cord is made by twisting many (   )s together, so it is very strong.
5. Let's (   ) the vegetable garden with a high wire fence to keep out the deer.
6. Many companies are hoping to get the building contract for the new park, so the (   ) is very tough.
7. In their anger the (   )s burned the main government building to the ground.
8. That low steady (   ) means the dog is angry. Please be careful.
9. Because of the earthquake, we had to live in (   ) housing, which was very uncomfortable.
10. The child hoped to become a great (   ) of piano music, like Chopin.

> rebel, temporary, competition, surround, soothing, universal, composer, bow, growling, thread

Chapter 8 —— Music   59

4 First Viewing: "What is Music?"

Watch the videoclip.

5 True or False: videoclip

Listen to each sentence. Check true (T) or false (F).

1. T ☐ F ☐
2. T ☐ F ☐
3. T ☐ F ☐
4. T ☐ F ☐
5. T ☐ F ☐

6 All that Jazz: listening tips

1. Stress can lead to stress

Listen to the following 3 dialogues and try to guess the single reason that **B** has completely misunderstood **A** each time. (If you don't know, please be patient)

1) **A**: She can swim very well.

   B: Then why was she given the job? Obviously we need a good swimmer.

2) **A**: He can meet you after work this evening.

   B: Oh, too bad. I was hoping we could talk this evening. When is he available?

3) **A**: You can eat anything at all for dinner. It's your birthday.

   B: What! Eating nothing is not a good birthday present!

Here is a hint: **A** is a Japanese learner of English, and **B** is a native English speaker, and the problem is one of pronunciation.

The problem: You have probably seen this kind of list: **man / pan / can / can't /**, right? Have you been told that the /a/ sound is the same in each case? In the above 3 sentences, did you hear "can" as on this list? If so, that's the reason **B** didn't understand you. Are you surprised?

In a simple list, the /a/ in "can" and "can't" are the same, but not in spoken sentences. Because of English rhythm, the word "can't" is stressed and the /a/ is full and clear like in "man", but "can" is <u>not</u> stressed, but "reduced", and sounds like /kn/. Also, native speakers don't say the /t/ in "can't" strongly, and sometimes it is not heard at all. Therefore, **B** heard "can't" when **A** said "can", and so **B** understood the opposite of what **A** intended!!!

60   Getting Personal

2. *Read the following dialogues stressing "can't" but reducing the stress in "can". Then Listen.*

a) **A**: You can use international credit cards in any of the airport shops.
   B: That's excellent! This airport is very modern and convenient.

b) **A**: It seems the new clerk can't type and can't do simple math.
   B: Is that so! I'll fire him tomorrow morning, first thing.

3. *Imagine that **A** in #1 does not put stress on "can". **B** will now understand **A** better and answer differently. Rewrite **B**'s answers and practice the dialogues in pairs. Then listen.*

7 Second Viewing

Watch the videoclip again.

8 Comprehension Check: videoclip

Write an answer for each question.

1. What does Clara do in the morning before leaving for work?

2. What are some of the things the students heard during the performance of the piano piece? Mention at least one.

3. What is Clara's final understanding of what music is?

4. What does the haiku of Basho teach us?

9 Dictation

Listen and complete each sentence.

1. There are (   ) (   ), and (   ) (   ) (   ) (   ) (   ) song (   ) (   ) (   ), and the sound of the wind blowing through the trees.
2. After (   ) (   ) (   ) (   ), the performer (   ) (   ), bowed, (   ) (   ) (   ) (   ) (   ).
3. We live (   ) (   ) (   ) (   ) (   ) (   ) (   ) silence.

10 Useful Expressions

Complete each sentence with the appropriate word.

1. The joy he felt when his son was born, was of a (   ) that he had never experienced before.
    A. nature　　B. fact　　C. dream　　D. grade
2. (   ) to the contributions of many people, we are able to buy gifts for the poor children.
    A. Owed　　B. Thanks　　C. Taking　　D. Up
3. Beethoven composed his 9th Symphony when he was completely deaf. This is proof (   ) his genius.
    A. to　　B. of　　C. with　　D. about
4. Italian is like music (   ) my ears.
    A. to　　B. against　　C. into　　D. by

11 Take Five: let's take a break

Music Trivia Quiz

The items on the left have some connection with the items on the right, but they are in jumbled order. Join them to make reasonable pairs.

1. Namie Amuro   woodwind
2. Seiji Ozawa   Take Five
3. red shoes   Can you celebrate?
4. Avril Lavigne   A Whole New World
5. John Lennon   Innocent World
6. Dave Brubeck   Canada
7. Vivaldi   Japanese harp
8. the musical "Chicago"   All That Jazz
9. koto   deaf
10. a capella   Thriller
11. bassoon   Imagine
12. Mr. Children   Four Seasons
13. Beethoven   Yokohama
14. Aladdin   conductor
15. Michael Jackson   unaccompanied voice

12 Expansion Questions

1. Often music is associated in our lives with experiences we've had, or important memories. Can you think of a case in your own life where this is true? Explain.
2. The introductory reading tells how music keeps the spirits of the Acholi people alive. Can you think of other situations where music (and the other arts) have the power to affect us deeply? Are there any negative effects of music?

Chapter 9

Gender and Language:
hidden sexism

1 Introductory Reading

Read the passage below.

Easily Tricked

We are in a period of transition in terms of gender awareness. Not so long ago, the sentence, "Somebody forgot his pen", would have passed unnoticed, but we now consider "his" to be sexist when referring to either gender. We try to avoid it although the alternatives ("his/her", "her/his", singular "their", etc.) feel troublesome. Feminist efforts have helped reveal the strong male feeling in words like "his", whatever their usage. It would seem easy to avoid these sexist words, but we often forget, as we see in this chapter's videoclip.

Now consider this sentence. "Three customers at the restaurant were chattering and being really silly." Do you feel the three could be male beer-drinking wrestlers? Probably not. What if someone told you that gossipy nurses were complaining about the chief doctor's powerful and aggressive manner? Would you imagine male nurses and a female chief doctor? No, right? Vocabulary such as "silly", "chatter", and "gossipy" is associated with females, and "powerful" and "aggressive", with males. Also, we continue to assume that nurses are women and chief doctors, men.

The fact is, society is still sexist, and we are easily tricked by the gender conditioning we've grown up with, so sometimes gender bias in language is difficult to notice. However, people are getting better at it.

Focusing on gender in language reveals a lot about society because of the inseparable connection between language and culture. Growing gender awareness is bringing positive changes to both society and language, but we are a long way from true equality. We must continue working hard to achieve both a gender-free society and gender-free language.

(277 words)

2 True or False: Introductory Reading

Answer true (T) or false (F).

1. Using "his" for both females and males used to be common. (　)
2. Some words, like "silly" and "powerful", tend to feel gender-specific. (　)
3. There is a very close link between language and culture. (　)

3 Vocabulary Check

Fill in the blanks with the words below.

1. The (　　) from childhood to adulthood is not always very smooth in these complex times.
2. The plane will soon (　　) in New York. Please fasten your seat belts.
3. This company is (　　) because women aren't paid equally.
4. The chimpanzees were taught to (　　) the balls according to color.
5. This public bath shows (　　) in that it refuses foreigners.
6. In many professional sports a certain amount of (　　) behavior is expected.
7. The mother told the child that it is bad manners to (　　) people when they're speaking.
8. Listen to these tapes of the meeting. I think they (　　) a major scandal.
9. I know about the surprise party, but I'll (　　) I don't know.
10. The learners have difficulty with many Japanese (　　)s intended to show politeness.

> transition, sexist, reveal, aggressive, bias, pretend, term, categorize, interrupt, land

4 First Viewing: "Gender Language"

Watch the videoclip.

Notes   ordeal：試練

5 True or False: videoclip

Listen to each sentence . Check true (T) or false (F).

1.   T ☐   F ☐
2.   T ☐   F ☐
3.   T ☐   F ☐
4.   T ☐   F ☐
5.   T ☐   F ☐

6 All that Jazz: listening tips

Questions: Up and Down

INTRODUCTION TO THE EXERCISE: *Read the following aloud:*

Did you notice in the videoclip that Aiko asked many questions? What kinds of questions were they? Were there any *Yes/No* questions? How about *WH* questions? Did the intonation go up? Down? How much did you learn about this sort of thing in school, and how much do you remember?

By the way, have you noticed yet, that this introduction section is entirely in questions? So, do you know what kind of tone to end each question with? Would you like a little help? In other words, what are the basic rules of "intonation" when asking questions? Do you remember that in *Yes/No* questions you end with an up tone? (Did you use the up tone just now?) OK, how about *WH* questions? Do you remember that *WH* questions end in a down tone?

O.K., how about *either/or* questions? In the first paragraph above, I asked, "Did the intonation go up? Down?" Each one of those questions is a *Yes/No* question, right? If those two questions were combined into one, how would you read it? Do you want to try it? "Should the intonation go up or down?" What is the basic intonation rule for *either/or* questions such as that one? Did you go up, and then down, as you should

68   Getting Personal

have?

You're probably getting bored with all this, but, how would you feel if your teacher told you to read the instructions one more time? Would you agree with him that it's a good idea? . . . . OOOooooops . . . . . . **Did you notice my mistake???!!!!!**
. . . . SORRY . .
. . . . Hmmm . . . OK
. . . ready to try it again?

EXERCISE:
Well . . . . time's up . . . There will be no exercise today.
. . . . SORRY . .

7 Second Viewing

Watch the videoclip again.

8 Comprehension Check: videoclip

Write an answer for each question.

1. Why do we use the term "Ms." nowadays?

2. What is the current term for housewife?

3. Why didn't Ms. Takahashi get angry at Jake?

4. Why did Scott blow the whistle in the end?

9 Dictation

Listen and complete each sentence.

1. Anyway, (   ) (   ) (   ) (   ) flight attendant (   ) (   ) (   ) (   ) (   ).
2. These days (   ) (   ) (   ) (   ) (   ) (   ) from (   ) (   ), (   ) and (   ).
3. Well, (   ) happened (   ) (   ) (   )?

10 Useful Expressions

Complete each sentence with the appropriate word.

1. The movie is good in (   ) of story line, but the camera work is terrible.
   - **A.** means
   - **B.** terms
   - **C.** forms
   - **D.** ways
2. The boss greeted me very casually, and said, "How's it (   )?"
   - **A.** on
   - **B.** going
   - **C.** doing
   - **D.** up
3. We had many problems, but everything worked (   ) well in the end.
   - **A.** around
   - **B.** up
   - **C.** out
   - **D.** off
4. He almost (   ) out, but recovered when we gave him some water.
   - **A.** brought
   - **B.** passed
   - **C.** died
   - **D.** took

11 Take Five: let's take a break

Hidden in the following letter grid (across, down, and diagonally from left to right) are many jobs. How many you can find? List them as gender-free words or gender-specific words.

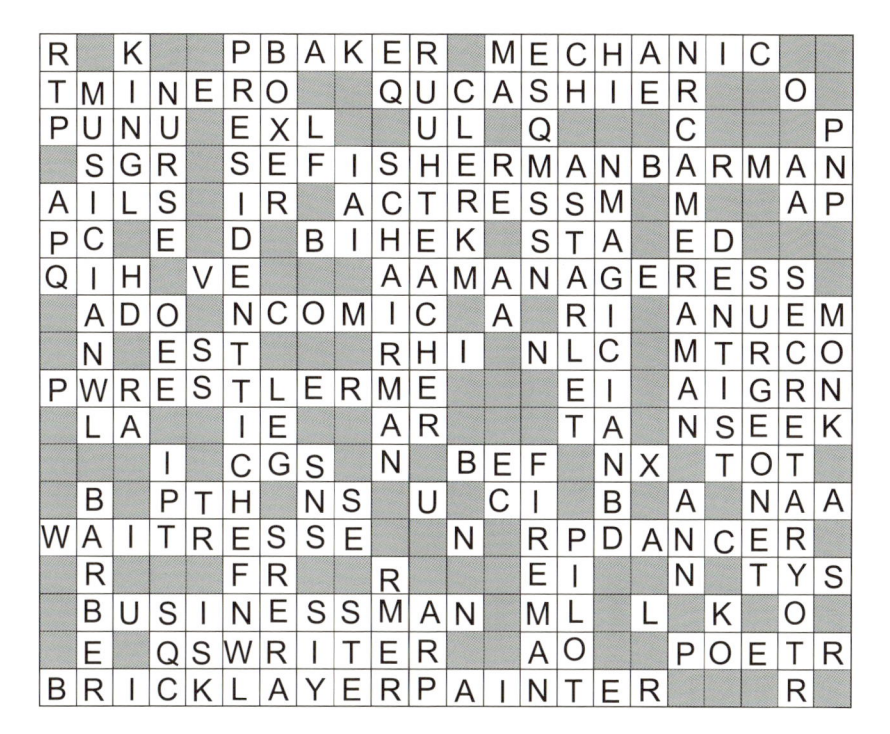

```
R  K     P B A K E R     M E C H A N I C
T M I N E R O     Q U C A S H I E R     O
P U N U   E X L     U L   Q       C       P
  S G R   S E F I S H E R M A N B A R M A N
A I L S   I R   A C T R E S S M   M     A P
P C   E   D   B I H E K   S T A   E D
Q I H   V E     A A M A N A G E R E S S
  A D O   N C O M I C   A   R I   A N U E M
  N   E S T       R H I   N L C   M T R C O
P W R E S T L E R M E       E I   A I G R N
  L A     I E   A R       T A   N S E E K
        I   C G S   N   B E F   N X   T O T
    B   P T H   N S   U   C I   B   A   N A A
W A I T R E S S E     N   R P D A N C E R
  R       F R     R       E I     N   T Y S
  B U S I N E S S M A N   M L   L   K   O
  E   Q S W R I T E R     A O     P O E T R
B R I C K L A Y E R P A I N T E R       R
```

Gender-free   Gender-specific

12 Expansion Questions

1. Do you feel that there is gender bias in the Japanese language? If so, give some examples.
2. In your view, how much of our sense of maleness and femaleness is natural from birth, and how much is learned in our culture?

Newspapers:
different roles

Chapter 10

1 Introductory Reading

Read the passage below.

Touching the Surface

Electronic media fascinates us, but we continue to love the old-fashioned newspaper. For many, like Adrian in the videoclip, the day is incomplete without it. What can be more relaxing than the morning paper and a steamy cup of coffee? We also expect to be informed, but is the average newspaper a reliable window on the world?

The mainstream media is often criticized for merely touching the surface of the "news", a select sampling of world events. Obviously limited space demands choices, but how are choices made . . . how is the news filtered?

Why, for example, are human rights abuses in China, big news, but stories of union leaders murdered by hired killers in Columbia's Coca Cola factory, not news? Such cases are documented in public government reports, but most people get their news from the mainstream media. By the way, Coke is a major media sponsor.

The use of statistics, a powerful tool, should also be examined carefully. Japanese newspapers report, for example, that there is 80% support for the death penalty. However, we are not told much about this 80%. If many of these people have carefully examined this complex issue, the statistic means one thing. If not, it means something completely different. Therefore we really should be told more.

The newspaper with its wide and varied readership, could be a place for discussion of difficult issues. Democracy guarantees us the right to hold any opinion without fear, but it isn't much of a democracy if we forget that our opinions have consequences. In a healthy democracy, freedom and responsibility are inseparable partners, and the newspaper is a vital tool.

(272 words)

2 True or False: Introductory Reading

Answer true (T) or false (F).

1. Many people like to read the newspaper in the morning. (   )
2. Mainstream newspapers always deal with events in great depth. (   )
3. Because statistics are clear, they don't have to be explained in great detail. (   )

3 Vocabulary Check

Fill in the blanks with the words below.

1. The (   )s of newspaper articles are usually short and can be read quickly.
2. This story is about a poor girl who marries into a (   ) family.
3. In the U.S., "pants" means trousers, but in Britain it means (   ) for men.
4. Even though there are many laws to enforce equality of men and women, women are still (   )d against.
5. The U.S. government is (   )d for its lack of concern for environmental problems.
6. There are many responsibilities connected with this job. We need someone who is (   ) and honest.
7. *Amnesty International* publicizes human rights (   )s around the world.
8. I'm not good at numbers, so I find (   ) difficult to understand.
9. One of the (   )s of buying the house was they each had to take a second job.
10. Life is about taking risks. Nobody can (   ) anything about the future.

> reliable, abuse, statistics, guarantee, consequence, headline criticize, underwear, discriminate, royal

4 First Viewing: "Newspapers in Britain"

Watch the videoclip.

Notes   tabloid：タブロイド紙

5 True or False: videoclip

Listen to each sentence . Check true (T) or false (F).

1. T ☐   F ☐
2. T ☐   F ☐
3. T ☐   F ☐
4. T ☐   F ☐
5. T ☐   F ☐

6 All that Jazz: listening tips

New Information

One reason for stress in spoken English is to indicate "new" information.

EXAMPLE: "She bought me **flowers** . . . **beautiful** flowers."

1. *In the video, Adrian says,* "**I love reading newspapers**. . . . Do **you** like newspapers **too**? I wonder what **kind** of newspapers you like to read, and **how** you read them." *The stressed words (in bold) are "new information".*

Read the following silly conversation aloud in pairs. It's between 6-year old, Miriam, and her older brother, Philip. Natural stress points are in bold print. Then listen.

Miriam: I'm **hungry**.

 Philip: You **just ate**.

Miriam: I ate **hours** ago.

 Philip: Do you want a **banana**?

Miriam: I **don't want** a dumb banana!

 Philip: **What do** you want?

Miriam: I want some **coconut pudding**.

76   Getting Personal

Philip: It's **not good** for you.

Miriam: It **is**. It's made of **milk**.

Philip: It's got **lots** of **sugar** in it.

Miriam: Well, it's **delicious**.

Philip: **Anyway**, there **isn't** any.

Miriam: There **is**. **Mom made** some **yesterday**.

       (*She looks for it*) **Where is** it?

       Did **Mom** eat it?

Philip: She **doesn't like** creamy things.

Miriam: Maybe **Dad** ate it.

Philip: He's **fat** so he's on a **diet**.

Miriam: Ohhhh . . . **you** ate it!

2. Read this conversation aloud in pairs, adding stress where you think it fits (Some sounds that are stressed based on different stress rules, are already marked). Then listen.

Paul: Where's the newspaper?

Freda: Which newspaper?

Paul: *The Guardian*. **I just** bought it.

Freda: I bought *The Independent*.

Paul: Well, where did you put it?

Freda: On the table.

Paul: Which table?

Freda: The kitchen table.

Paul: So did **I**.

Freda: (*in her mind*: Ah, **I wish** I could just **sit down**

       and **read** the **paper** with a **nice cup** of **coffee**.)

       Where are the coffees?

Paul: I poured us coffee about 2 minutes ago.

Freda: Well, where did you put them?

Paul: I put them on the kitchen table,

       We always drink them there.

Freda: Well, **maybe** they're **still there**.

Paul: Uh ... they **are**, next to the newpapers.

7   Second Viewing

Watch the videoclip again.

8 Comprehension Check: videoclip

Write an answer for each question.

1. Why does Adrian read *The Guardian*?

2. What are tabloid articles mostly about?

3. What are some standard news topics about Japan in British newspapers?

4. What is one example Adrian gives of a strange story about Japan?

9 Dictation

Listen and complete each sentence.

1. In fact, (   ) (   ) (   ) (   ) (   ) unless I have (   ) (   ).
2. (   ) (   ) long (   ) cover (   ) wide (   ) (   ) (   ).
3. This story tells how difficult it (   ) (   ) for (   ) (   ) (   ) (   ) (   ) (   ) in Japan.

78   Getting Personal

10 Useful Expressions

Complete each sentence with the appropriate word.

1. He was not (   ) of a musician, but he was an eager music teacher.
   A. much　　B. kind　　C. type　　D. talent
2. I won't go (   ) you go with me.
   A. instead　　B. otherwise　　C. whether　　D. unless
3. She (   ) visits the capital because she hates the noise and crowds.
   A. rarely　　B. frequently　　C. generally　　D. always
4. This game is a lot of (   ). You should try it sometime.
   A. joy　　B. fun　　C. play　　D. amazement

11 Take Five: let's take a break

Two Amazing Facts

A. *In each of the following sentences there are three choices. Choose the best one.*
   1. If you want a higher grade, you'll have to (waste / consume / produce) better work.
   2. It takes several (weeks / months / years) of education and training to become a doctor.
   3. Unfortunately, there are (scorpions / pigs / bees) in Okinawa, but, at least, there are none elsewhere in Japan.
   4. Quebec is famous for its maple (syrup / honey / milk) which has become quite popular in Japan.
   5. She loves to begin her day with a nice, hot (teaspoon / ton / cup) of coffee and some toast.

B. *Use this chart to place the 10 words you didn't use in A.*
   (2 creatures) _____ _____
   (2 amounts) _____ _____
   (2 time periods) _____ _____
   (2 verbs) _____ _____
   (2 foods) _____ _____

C. *You will now find out 2 very amazing facts. Use the words in the chart in **B** to complete the two short texts below.*

1. These little creatures, (a   ), spend their whole working lives, only three (b   ), producing just one (c   ) of delicious (d   ). It is a natural sugar product that's very sweet, and we often (e   ) one little worker's full production in one happy mouthful.

2. Japan throws away about 20 million (a   )s of unused food yearly. That's 5 million every 3 (b   ) . . . everything from junkfood to basic things like rice and (c   ). In 2007, the amount (d   )d was 5 times more than the amount given to the world's poor in food aid. Some of this food is now recycled to feed farm animals, mainly (e   ).

D. *What do you think of these little stories? Do you know any similar amazing facts?*

12 Expansion Questions

1. Do you try to keep up with the news? Where do you get your news and what topics interest you the most, or the least?
2. Adrian talks of "quality" and "tabloid" newspapers in Britain. How is it in Japan? What are the merits and demerits of revealing the private lives of politicians and celebrities?

Chapter 11

Art:
all about life

1 Introductory Reading

Read the passage below.

Life and Art

Picasso continues to inspire us, often in surprising ways, as we see in the videoclip, but where did he himself find inspiration? Everywhere. Life and art for him were so connected that one flowed easily into the other. He said, "The artist is a receptacle for emotions that come from all over the place: from the sky, from the earth, from a scrap of paper, from a passing shape, from a spider's web."

The foolishness of humankind was also a source of ideas for Picasso. He was asked to do a large painting for the Spanish Pavilion at the 1937 World's Fair in Paris, but he hesitated for three months waiting for the right moment. It came with the news on April 27, 1937 that the little Spanish village of Guernica, was now in bloody ruin because the Nazis had used it for bombing practice. Picasso, outraged, began his painting, "Guernica", using black and white to express the horror shown in newspaper photos.

During World War Two, Picasso lived in Nazi-occupied Paris. One day, the Gestapo, who harassed him constantly, visited his apartment, and one officer, noticing a photo of his Guernica, asked, "Did you do that?" Picasso responded, "No, you did."

Clearly Picasso lived the spirit of his own words. He said, "One must act in painting as in life, directly." He also said, "Art is a lie that makes us realize the truth." The disturbing images in his Guernica have become universally familiar as symbols of the tragedy of war, and are a stronger dedication to peace than a million speeches ever could be. (272 words)

2 True or False: Introductory Reading

Answer true (T) or false (F).

1. Picasso was inspired by everything, even simple everyday things. (　)
2. The Nazis bombed Guernica, but there was not too much damage. (　)
3. Picasso gave many speeches dedicated to universal peace. (　)

3 Vocabulary Check

Fill in the blanks with the words below.

1. I still sometimes feel (　　) with my English, but I guess I'm getting a little better.
2. The teacher shows a deep (　　) for the students, so they feel at ease expressing their concerns.
3. Her reading level was very (　　) but her speaking ability was quite high.
4. Martin Luther King's speech was a moving (　　) to freedom and democracy.
5. My teacher's positive comments about my paper really helped to build my (　　).
6. The Niagra falls are a (　　) natural sight; one of the most beautiful in Canada.
7. Even though the tigers were in their cage, when they began to (　　), we were terrified.
8. The little girl's laughter and silly (　　) cheered up the old man.
9. The student was so (　　) with the grade that we were worried she'd attack the teacher.
10. This beautiful movie is one example of the director's exceptional (　　).

> outraged, dedication, tenderness, roar, elementary, playfulness, creativity, magnificent, confidence, frustrated

Chapter 11 —— Art 83

4 First Viewing: "On Art"

Watch the videoclip.

vibrant：活気に満ちた

5 True or False: videoclip

Listen to each sentence. Check true (T) or false (F).

1. T☐ F☐
2. T☐ F☐
3. T☐ F☐
4. T☐ F☐
5. T☐ F☐

6 All that Jazz: listening tips

"Quotes are stressed," she said

Look at the title. The part, "Quotes are stressed", **is** stressed, (said in a higher tone than "she said"). It's as though a narrator is highlighting the quoted part. The rule is the same in sentences that include words like "I believe", "I think", etc.

  EXAMPLE: **The rainy season**, I think, **will end tomorrow.**

Perhaps this stress rule is easier to understand if we say something very dramatic.

  EXAMPLE: "**Aaaaah . . . .** " she cried out, "**I just stepped on broken glass!!!**"

However, the rule is true in undramatic cases also.

  EXAMPLE: "**I'll take a shower,**" he thought, "**and then get dressed.**"

Try saying the following sentences on the topic of art:

1. "**This painting is colorful,**" the critic said, "**but it lacks power.**"

2. **Picasso**, I believe, **inspires people with his words as well as his art**.

HOWEVER, if the "narrator" part ("She said", "I think", etc.) is at the beginning of the sentence, it is said with more stress.

  EXAMPLE: **I think the rainy season will end tomorrow.**

84 Getting Personal

EXERCISE:
Practice reading the following passage aloud using stress as explained above. Then listen.

Picasso the Wordsmith

"I am always doing that which I cannot do," Picasso said, "in order that I may learn how to do it." These words, I believe, should encourage students to take chances when they speak English so they can learn from their mistakes.

Another time he said, "I begin with an idea and then it becomes something else." I think these words are also inspiring for Japanese learners of English. Picasso means, I think, that we can't always plan everything ahead. Sometimes we discover things in unexpected ways. Students often try to form perfect sentences in their heads before saying anything. Spending less time practicing silently, I believe, would build flexibility. How can we encourage students to take more risks, I wonder.

7 Second Viewing

Watch the videoclip again.

8 Comprehension Check: videoclip

Write an answer for each question.

1. Why is Clara attracted to the painting of a jumping child?

2. What painting did Clara's art teacher show the students?

3. What frustrated Clara as she watched Picasso paint?

4. Why does Clara say mistakes are good?

9 Dictation

Listen and complete each sentence.

1. (   ) (   ) (   ) soft (   ) between (   ) (   ) and (   ) (   ) and that's what attracts me.
2. I loved Ms. Rubin because (   ) (   ) (   ) (   ) freedom (   ) paint as we pleased.
3. We don't see the struggle (   ) (   ) artist (   ) (   ) (   ) (   ) creating.

10 Useful Expressions

Complete each sentence with the appropriate word.

1. In spite of the dangers, they (   ) to climb Mt. Fuji in the winter.
    A. challenged   **B.** dared   **C.** risked   **D.** adventured
2. We shouldn't say "no" (   ) higher taxes if they're for a good reason.
    A. on   **B.** at   **C.** around   **D.** to
3. It was her courage (   ) moved me.
    A. that   **B.** what   **C.** one   **D.** did
4. This task is difficult, but (   ) a chance. I'm sure you can do it.
    A. get   **B.** have   **C.** take   **D.** choose

11 Take Five: let's take a break

How many words?

The word "artistic" has 8 letters. If we use any of those letters, in any order, we can make many new words. Here are a few: sat / start / star / attic / rat / rats / art

Using the letters in the words below, make as many English words as you can.

masterpiece:

paintings:

creativity:

12 Expansion Questions

1. There are three quotations by Picasso in the introductory reading. Choose one and give your explanation and opinion about it. What is the importance of the arts in your own life?
2. Some say that, generally speaking, creativity is not encouraged enough in Japan. Do you agree? Give your thoughts on this matter.

Information Technology:
finding a balance

Chapter 12

1 Introductory Reading

Read the passage below.

Cutting Carrots with a Chainsaw

In these digital times we are easily fascinated by technology's ability to do things at super speed and efficiency. Bill Gates, who helped shape this era, has interesting thoughts to share on the subject in the videoclip. Here though, we'll look at it from another perspective, that of our senses.

Take email for instance. Clearly it is brilliant for sending messages to many people instantly, effortlessly, and cheaply. However, we use it always and for everything, even to write long, leisurely letters to our closest friends, a task it simply is unsuited for. It's like cutting carrots with a chainsaw. A visit to the Heian Era will help demonstrate why.

Imagine it's 1000AD. You're under a tree, writing a letter on beautiful paper in fine script; decorating it with fragrant flowers. Using all your senses, you balance the colors and textures lovingly. When all the senses are awake, the process of composing a friendly letter is greatly improved. This awareness is one of Japan's gifts to the world. Today, however, the pleasure of such a simple act is almost lost because it takes time, which is something we try to avoid. We choose instead to ruin our eyes in front of an electronic screen while all our other senses go to sleep because they are not needed.

The real problem is that we choose the quick, convenient way, automatically. We forget that sometimes it's better to slow down and put our modern tools aside. Until we recognize when we should do that, we are no better than slaves, to both our machines and to ourselves.

(265 words)

2 True or False: Introductory Reading

Answer true (T) or false (F).

1. According to the writer, email is the best way to write letters to our friends. (   )
2. In the Heian Period, writing a letter involved all our senses. (   )
3. The writer feels we should never choose the quick, convenient way. (   )

3 Vocabulary Check

Fill in the blanks with the words below.

1. A close (   ) of mine, an aunt, moved to Sweden. I'm looking forward to visiting her this summer.
2. Many choose margarine as a (   ) for butter because it contains no animal fat.
3. There was a (   ) smell of roses in the perfume factory.
4. So many advances have been made in information technology in such a short time. It is really (   ).
5. If the number of polar bear continues to (   ) at this rate, they will become extinct.
6. We can (   ) to the conservation of forests by carrying our own chopsticks.
7. The conference was held in Kyoto to discuss how to combat (   ) warming.
8. Children educated in foreign schools away from home sometimes suffer a loss of (   ).
9. Many children spend hours alone playing video games. This (   ) can be psychologically harmful.
10. It is difficult for small ethnic groups to (   ) their traditions because of modernization.

> fragrant, global, identity, relative, contribute, preserve, diminish, substitute, incredible, phenomenon

Chapter 12 — Information Technology

4 First Viewing: "An Interview with Bill Gates"

Watch the videoclip.

5 True or False

Listen to each sentence. Check true (T) or false (F).

1. T ☐ F ☐
2. T ☐ F ☐
3. T ☐ F ☐
4. T ☐ F ☐
5. T ☐ F ☐

6 All that Jazz: listening tips

Conversational Oral English

Bill Gates, in the interview, uses conversational, spontaneous English, full of "fillers" or "hesitations", so we hear repetitions, relaxed grammar, non-word sounds, and words such as "look", "you know", "sort of", "like", "I mean", etc. that lose their usual meaning. They add effect, but are not essential to the basic meaning of the sentence, and tend to not be stressed.

EXAMPLES:

1. <u>Look</u>, I know you're angry, but I said I was, <u>you know</u>, sorry.
2. I'm <u>sort of</u> busy right now, so, <u>like</u>, could you call me later?
3. He seems really nice, but, <u>I mean</u>, what do you think?
4. <u>Ummmm</u>, let me guess . . . <u>uhh</u>, sorry, I have no idea.
5. <u>Wha what</u> do you mean? Are <u>you you</u> serious!?

EXERCISE:

1. *Find such features of conversational English in this excerpt from the Bill Gates interview, and underline them. Then listen.*

   "And so by doing, you know, video meetings in business, you get you know you get uhhh get home earlier and and be there face-to-face with your kids.

92 Getting Personal

So you'll strike a balance. I mean you know, this is a country where people send more greeting cards than any country in the world. You know that's not face-to-face."

2. *In review, the words "look", "you know", "sort of", "like", "I mean", have both a "real" meaning and a "conversational" meaning. These words are underlined in the following sentences. Indicate, above each underlined word, whether their "real" meaning is intended (R), or their conversational meaning (C). Read the sentences aloud. Then listen.*

1. Look at the squirrel in the maple tree over there. It's so cute.

2. Why would he, I mean, say a thing like that? He's usually very nice.

3. Her voice is sort of, not very good. She, like, sounds like a sick cat.

4. I think you know exactly what to do. Please get started immediately!

5. Like jazz and classical music are my favorite. What sort of music do you like?

6. Look stop complaining. You're not, you know, a little baby.

7. I always say what I mean. Why would I, like, lie to you?

7 Second Viewing

Watch the videoclip again.

Chapter 12 —— Information Technology   93

8 Comprehension Check: videoclip

Write an answer for each question.

1. What were people afraid of when books became available?

___

2. How do workers at Microsoft Development Center stay connected with their own countries? Mention at least one.

___

3. In what way does the computer reduce the need to travel for business?

___

4. How does the computer affect family life?

___

9 Dictation

Listen and complete each sentence.

1. That's, people talk about that a lot, you know, the question is (   ) (   ) (   ) (   ) a tool, how (   ) (   ) (   ) (   )?
2. They're (   ) (   ) back (   ) (   ) (   ) and (   ) (   ) (   ) with (   ) through the Internet.
3. We have (   ) (   ) to (   ) (   ) (   ) (   ).

94 Getting Personal

10 Useful Expressions

Complete each sentence with the appropriate word.

1. Let's (   ) aside our differences and try to be more flexible.
   A. stay   B. put   C. keep   D. pull
2. Although she flies a lot, she is (   ) anxious this time about flying in such a small plane.
   A. something   B. anything   C. somewhat   D. anyhow
3. It's necessary to (   ) a balance between work and pleasure because both are necessary.
   A. strike   B. join   C. do   D. leave
4. When I leave Japan, I hope we'll continue to stay (   ) touch.
   A. in   B. on   C. at   D. with

11 Take Five: let's take a break

Certain vocabulary mistakes result when an incorrect form of a root word is used. Often it is nouns, adjectives, adverbs, and verbs that get mixed up. Find such mistakes in the text below and correct them.

EXAMPLES:
1. I am not <u>interesting</u> in math, but we have to take this course. (> interested)
2. My secretary is very <u>efficiency</u> and my desk is always very neat. (> efficient)

The mysterious gourmet snack

Hiro moved to a new town and was very pleasant about it. The area was convenience and also very excited because there was a various of international shops that were very sophistication and chic. He also felt safety because his neighborhood was such a kindness and gentleness old woman, and was always ready to help him with little things. She asked Hiro to call her by her personal name, Yumiko.

One day Yumiko invited him for tea, and they sat down in her prettiness kitchen together. On the table was a plate with some kind of strangeness sausage or something. Yumiko invited him to taste some, but it looked like parts of a died rat in a thickness

Chapter 12 —— Information Technology

white sauce. Hiro was so shocking and even a little worrying that it was a danger thing to eat. He was embarrassing and didn't know what to do. He didn't want to be rudeness.

"Don't be shyness," Yumiko said. "Please try some. I saw them make this recipe on a TV cooking show." Her softness smile made him feel more relaxing and he took a small piece. When he put it in his mouth he was very surprising because it tasted very, very well.

Many years later, Hiro's memory of this snack is still vividness. He feels he acted in a very silliness way because he didn't like trying new foods then. However, Yumiko's gourmet dish impressed him deeply, and taught him to be bravery about tasting unusually dishes. He loves to cook now and often prepares very luxury dishes for his family. His children think his food is weirdness and wish he would choice a different hobby.

12 Expansion Questions

1. Bill Gates discusses some of the benefits of information technology. What are the dangers or negative aspects of this technology?
2. Explain how the mobile phone has changed communication and other aspects of life. What are some of the problems connected with the mobile phone?

JPCA

日本出版著作権協会
http://www.jpca.jp.net/

本書は日本出版著作権協会（JPCA）が委託管理する著作物です。
複写（コピー）・複製、その他著作物の利用については、事前にJPCA（電話 03-3812-9424, e-mail:info@e-jpca.com）の許諾を得て下さい。なお、無断でコピー・スキャン・デジタル化等の複製をすることは著作権法上の例外を除き、著作権法違反となります。

▼写真提供
表紙（左上）© Losevsky Pavel／（右上）© Pennyimages／（左下）© Dash／（右下）© Phase4Photography
本文 p. 1, 9, 17, 25, 33, 41, 49, 57, 65, 73, 81, 89（上）© Clara Birnbaum ; p. 89（下）© ＡＦＰ＝時事

▼ビデオクリップ出演
Chapter　1. The Camping Trip: Ian Willey / Adrian Clarke
Chapter　2. A Year Off: Adrian Clarke
Chapter　3. Dear Wendy: Clara Birnbaum
Chapter　4. Counseling: Leandra Deeton / Elizabeth Lange
Chapter　5. Korea: Scott Berlin
Chapter　6. An Adventure in Bali: Clara Birnbaum
Chapter　7. One Woman's Experience: Aiko Thompson
Chapter　8. What is Music?: Clara Birnbaum
Chapter　9. Gender Language: Aiko Thompson / Scott Berlin
Chapter 10. Newspapers in Britain: Adrian Clarke
Chapter 11. On Art: Clara Birnbaum
Chapter 12. An Interview with Bill Gates: Bill Gates（聞き手：鳥飼玖美子）

Getting Personal Using Videoclips: Watch, Listen and Read
大学生のためのビデオクリップ英語総合学習

2009年 4 月 1 日　　初版発行
2016年 4 月10日　　第 6 刷発行

編著者　Clara Birnbaum／高山一郎

発行者　森　信久
発行所　株式会社　松柏社
　　　　〒102-0072　東京都千代田区飯田橋1-6-1
　　　　TEL 03 (3230) 4813（代表）
　　　　FAX 03 (3230) 4857
　　　　http://www.shohakusha.com
　　　　e-mail: info@shohakusha.com

装　幀　小島トシノブ＋齋藤四歩（NONdesign）
組　版　井澤俊二
印刷・製本　中央精版印刷株式会社
ISBN978-4-88198-618-9
略号＝618

Copyright © 2009 by C. Birnbaum, I. Takayama

本書を無断で複写・複製することを禁じます。
落丁・乱丁は送料小社負担にてお取り替え致します。